The Survival Guide to Retirement

<u>Retirement</u> – Noun *'The withdrawal from one's position or occupation or from one's active working life'. A person may also semi-retire by reducing work hours or workload.*

Forward

The time in life that every adult dreams of; not have to go to work, an endless period of free time in your life that has no boundaries, world cruises, endless travel or just many years of pottering around in the garden. Or is it? It can be everything you have ever dreamed of, or a complete nightmare. This book gives you the facts about retirement, on how to plan it, and hopefully how to survive it.

Retirement is a stage of life that does not just happen, to try to make it successful it must be planned years in advance and adequately financed through personal investment. It is not the same for everyone and is very much decided by the lifestyle you have chosen to live, medical conditions, family and lifetime choices along the way, and what others want and think you need. But ultimately it is time to be a little selfish, self-indulgent and get back what you have spent a lifetime planning for.

Ultimately this book will not have all the answers but will give you the facts to enable you to make informed judgements, to make your retirement as successful as possible. It will also answer questions that will be helpful as you step headlong into retirement.

Footnote – *Part One is best read when you are in your early 30's. The pre-planning is critical to a successful retirement.*

Accuracy of Information

The author has worked hard to make sure the information provided in this publication is as accurate as possible when published. No one is perfect and because of this no guarantees are made as to the completeness or accuracy of information in this publication. The author cannot be responsible for any changes to rules, laws etc.

Contents

2.4C. Social Media

2.4D. Artificial Intelligence

2.4E. Online Scams

2.4F. Technology Aids and Digital Home Assistants

In this part we look at the planning that should be carried out at the earliest opportunity in your working life. The retirement planning is the part that many people leave too late and subsequently end up with an inferior pension. It has been said that many young people have 3 life insurances in life, the first one they default on, the second they cash in, and the third they keep. Although no statistics exist it is possible that the same can possibly be said for personal pensions.

A few years ago, the UK Government in partnership with private investment companies created workplace pensions to run alongside the state pension system, these are now mandatory. Whatever pension you choose to adopt, make sure it is within you budget, you can always increase payment later in life, but starting it early is more important than the amount paid in.

1.1 Pension Planning

What is a pension plan?

A pension is long-term saving plan that you build up across your working life to create enough income for later life. They are designed to provide you with money in later life, most often when you are reducing or stopping work.

A pension is money you'll use to live on when you retire. Most people will get a state pension from the government which covers your basic needs. But it is also a clever idea to try and save some extra money in a pension fund, to give you a decent standard of living.

Your employer has to offer a workplace pension scheme by law. They must automatically enrol anyone who is eligible - this is called automatic enrolment.

Some people choose to think creatively and instead of a pension plan they buy property. The idea being that the property increases in value and when the time comes can be sold to fund their retirement. Considered a reasonably safe bet, buying property in a rising market can be a good move, and can gain rental income along the way. It does have its fallbacks; although unlikely, the property market might crash or drop, and all maintenance and legal costs during ownership will be incurred by the investor. Also depending on market and location when it comes to sell, it might not be as quick as one had bargained on. If you opt for this way of investing, make sure you have all the right insurances in place, and be aware of planned changes in the local property market such as new roads and large developments.

What are the 3 main types of pensions?

Defined contribution pension. Sometimes called a 'money purchase' pension or referred to as a pension pot, these schemes are quite common today.

Defined benefit pension. This type of pension scheme has declined in popularity.

State pension.

What is a workplace pension scheme?

A workplace pension scheme is a way of saving for your retirement through contributions deducted direct from your wages. Your employer may also make contributions to your pension through the scheme. If you are eligible for automatic enrolment, your employer has to make contributions into the scheme.

Most schemes will also provide other benefits, for example, support for your partner if you die.

There are two types of workplace pension schemes:

Occupational pensions.

Group personal pensions or stakeholder pensions.

Occupational pensions

Occupational pension schemes are set up by employers to provide pensions for their employees. There are two different types of occupational pensions.

Final salary schemes.

Money purchase schemes.

Final salary schemes

Final salary pension schemes can also be called defined benefit schemes. In a final salary scheme, your pension is linked to your salary while you are working, so it automatically increases as your pay rises. Your pension is based on your pay at retirement and the number of years you have been in the scheme. Your pension entitlement does not depend on the performance of the stock market or other investments.

In most final salary schemes, you pay a set percentage of your wages towards your pension fund and your employer pays the rest. This means it is usually an innovative idea to join a final salary scheme if your employer offers one. However, final salary schemes are becoming less common, and most employers no longer offer them.

Money purchase schemes

Money purchase schemes can also be called defined contribution schemes. The money you pay into the scheme is invested with the aim of giving you an amount of money when you retire. Your pension is based on the amount of money paid in and on how the investments have performed. You will usually pay a percentage of your wages into the scheme and your employer may also pay a regular amount in, but this is not always the case. However, your employer may have to offer you automatic enrolment into a workplace pension, in which case they will be obliged to make contributions.

If you are offered a money purchase scheme through the workplace, it can be a promising idea to join if your employer makes contributions. However, if your employer is not going to make any contributions to the pension or you are not yet eligible for automatic enrolment, you may want to compare the benefits of the scheme with personal pensions schemes elsewhere.

For more information about personal pensions offered outside the workplace, look on the internet by searching 'choosing a personal pension.

The State Pension is a regular payment from the government most people can claim when they reach State Pension age. Your State Pension age depends on when you were born. You can find out your State Pension age by using the calculator on the GOV.UK website.

Increase in State Pension age from 66 to 67 under the Pensions Act 2014

The Pensions Act 2014 brought the increase in the State Pension age from 66 to 67 forward by 8 years. The State Pension age for both men and women will now increase to

67 between 2026 and 2028. The government also changed the way in which the increase in State Pension age is phased so that rather than reaching State Pension age on a specific date, people born between 6 April 1960 and 5 March 1961 will reach their State Pension age at 66 years and the specified number of months.

Increase in State Pension age from 67 to 68 under the Pensions Act 2007

Under the Pensions Act 2007 the State Pension age for both men and women will increase from 67 to 68 between 2044 and 2046.

The Pensions Act 2014 provides for a regular review of the State Pension age, at least once every 5 years. The review will be based around the idea that people should be able to spend a certain proportion of their adult life drawing a State Pension. The first review must be completed by May 2017. As well as life expectancy, it will consider a range of factors relevant to setting the pension age. After the review has reported, the government may then choose to bring forward changes to the State Pension age. Any proposals to do so would, like now, must go through Parliament before becoming law.

The government is not planning to revise the existing timetables for the equalisation of State Pension age to 65 or the rise in the State Pension age to 66 or 67. However the timetable for the increase in the State Pension age from 67 to 68 could change because of the review.

In the Autumn Statement on 5 December 2013, the Chancellor announced that this government believes that future generations should spend up to a third of their adult life in retirement. This principle implies that State Pension age should rise to 68 by the mid-2030s, and 69 by the late 2040s.

However, the government is not currently legislating for this change – these dates are indicative only, showing a general direction of travel for future State Pension age.

The amount of State Pension you will get depends on how many 'qualifying' years of National Insurance payments you have. This includes National Insurance contributions that you pay when you are working and contributions that are credited to you when you are unable to work.

You can get an estimate of how much State Pension you could get on GOV.UK. This is called a State Pension Statement.

How your State Pension will work depends on your age and gender and is paid to those who qualify by the Department of Work and Pensions (DWP).

It is important to remember that your state pension does not automatically get awarded to you. When you have reached or passed the qualifying age you must apply for your State Pension online. It will the take a few weeks before it is awarded, dependent on the workload at the time in the Department of Work and Pensions (DWP) State Pensions are then paid every for weeks into your bank account.

Currently increases are dictated by the rate of inflation published in the Consumer Price Index in September of each year. The increase is then implemented in the following April. This rule is not set in stone and can be changed periodically by the Government of the Day.

Getting qualifying years

The amount of State Pension you get depends on your National Insurance record. Your National Insurance record includes National Insurance contributions that you pay when you are working and contributions that are credited to you when you are unable to work.

For example, you can get National Insurance credits when you are claiming Employment and Support Allowance or Jobseeker's Allowance, or if you have caring responsibilities. Your record can also include voluntary contributions that you choose to pay to cover gaps when you are not working or getting credits.

When you reach State Pension age, you can claim a State Pension if you have paid or been credited with enough National Insurance contributions during your working life.

What you get depends on how many 'qualifying years' of National Insurance contributions you have. Each tax year (6 April to 5 April) that you pay or are credited with National Insurance contributions counts as a qualifying year, provided you earn or are credited with earnings of at least a minimum amount. This amount changes every year.

Making voluntary National Insurance contributions

If you do not have enough qualifying years to get a full State Pension, you may be able to make up gaps in your National Insurance contribution record by paying voluntary contributions.

There is a time limit for doing this. You can find out more about voluntary contributions and the time limits for paying them on GOV.UK.

Claiming State Pension while you work

You can choose to keep on working, whether paid or on a voluntary basis, while claiming your State Pension. Any money you earn will not affect your State Pension, but it may affect your entitlement to other benefits such as Pension Credit, Housing Benefit and Council Tax Reduction (help with your rates in Northern Ireland).

The Money Advice Service

The Money Advice Service is a free, independent service. Their website has useful information about all types of pensions including a pension calculator for working out how much pension you will need. Go to www.moneyadviceservice.org.uk Other free advice is available from Pension Wise. Go to www.moneyhelper.org.uk

State Pension Deferment

A little-known area of pensions is the State Pension deferment scheme. After retirement age has passed the state pension does not have to be drawn at once and can be deferred in 12-month blocks. For ever year that it is deferred then the gross amount payable increases by 10% each year.

1.3 Retirement Planning

What is Retirement Planning?

Retirement planning means preparing today for your future life so that you continue to meet all your goals and dreams independently.

This includes setting your retirement goals, estimating the amount of money you will need, and investing to grow your retirement savings. Every retirement plan is unique.

It is good to start a plan early and at the same time enrol an Independent Financial Adviser (IFA) to help you. An IFA will help you to invest your money wisely to make the most of what assets and pensions that you have. During the advisory period, the IFA will offer you various financial illustrations relating to how your money could be invested. The IFA also has an obligation to inform you of how much they will earn from you taking up the advice and buying into the schemes that they recommend.

A good start to find an IFA is at the Unbiased website. Go to www.unbiased.co.uk

When to Retire

Employers used to be able to force workers to retire at 65 (*known as the Default Retirement Age*), but this law was scrapped in April 2011, following a campaign by Age UK. This means that you can keep working beyond 65 if you want or need to.

There is no legal requirement to retire in the UK, although the State Pension has defined start ages, that are dictated by your year of birth. The actual date that you start your retirement is entirely your choice. However, in recent years many employers will actively try and get you to delay your retirement. The bottom line is retirement is a combination when you can afford to and when you want to.

How do I know when it is time to retire in the UK?

How do you know when it is time to retire? 7 tell-tale signs

- You can afford to.
- You have something else to do.
- You are no longer supporting kids or parents.
- You are at the retirement age (or older)
- Is affecting your health.
- Your partner wants to retire too.
- It is time for you to relax.
- Or sadly, you have a terminal illness.

What is Estate Planning?

Your estate plan details your total assets, including your house, possessions, and accounts and how you would like these assets to be managed when you pass away.

A solicitor can be employed to aid you with estate planning, however there are many qualified small businesses that can recommend you and aid you for a fixed fee. You can also do all the groundwork yourself and complete you own estate planning at no cost. In the UK there is not a legal requirement to use a solicitor to create the documents that you need. Many documents are available in template format on the internet ready to be downloaded and completed. A small fee is often needed to download these templates.

There is still a legal requirement to get legal documents independently witnessed before they are stored. However, a common fault in creating your own will and other documents is not getting them signed and not telling relatives where they are stored.

What should be included in Estate Planning?

- Last Will and Testament.
- Nominating Executors of Your Will.
- Lasting Power of Attorney.
- Protected Will & Trusts.
- Inheritance Tax Planning.
- Care Fee Planning.
- Pre-Paid Funeral Planning.
- Secure Storage.

- An Ongoing Periodic Review.

What is Funeral Planning?

A funeral plan lets you pay in advance for some of your funeral, at today's prices. You can buy a plan from funeral directors and funeral plan providers. The money in the plan can only be used to pay for funeral costs. Dignity is one such company, but beware there may be minimum entry age levels, so best do your homework.

There are many large organisations in the UK that sell funeral bonds. These bonds are transferable throughout the UK and are normally index linked to ensure they grow in value and keep up with current prices. When buying one of these bonds, it is wise to ensure they are registered with The Financial Conduct Authority as well as being exactly what you need. If you can afford it, it makes good sense to pay for a funeral years in advance, locking in the price and saving your family money in later years. The bottom line is at some stage someone will have to pay the bill.

Planning a funeral can be overwhelming and stressful at a time when emotions are already high. Here are a few areas to help make it that little bit easier, the list is not endless, but at the end of the day you are paying so make sure it is what you want.

Funeral arrangements checklist:

- Look for funeral instructions written in the will.
- Check how the funeral will be paid for (whether totally by a funeral plan or other means).
- Ask for support from family members.
- Consider hiring a funeral director in advance.
- Choose a burial, cremation, or direct cremation.
- Decide on the coffin.
- Are cars to be included in the price.

2.1 When to Retire 'With All the Time in the World'

Nobody can recommend you on when to retire. In the UK there is no legal retirement age, and employers can no longer force their employees to retire at a particular age. It is up to you when you decide to stop working. Retirement is a state of living that you can phase in slowly, start at an early age, when your state pension is paid out, or it can be deferred until only you feel it is the right time. The majority of people when finances allow generally start working towards retirement a few years before a state pension is paid. That said there are no hard and fast rules for this, and only you can decide.

2.1A. Bucket Lists

By definition, a bucket list is "a few experiences or achievements that a person hopes to have or accomplish during their lifetime." For many years only people facing imminent death compiled a bucket list. More recently, since the expression has gained momentum, the meaning is thankfully less morbid. Many of us put off many dreams in life, saving them up for retirement.

Despite the heart-wrenching 2007 film 'The Bucket List' that starred Jack Nicholson and Morgan Freeman, you don't have to be dying to make a list of dreams. The origin of the term "bucket list" descends from the phrase "before you kick the bucket". Hence its first connotations that you're terminally ill if you make one. In recent years people start creating a bucket list in the early 50's.

Being realistic about bucket lists, to stand a chance of making them come true the need to be SMART. An acronym often used in business; *Specific, Achievable, Measurable, Relevant, and Time-Bound*. But most important of all in retirement, a bucket list needs to be affordable and within the limitation of your age-related physical state.

2.1B. Hobbies and Pastimes

A vitally important part of retirement is having worthwhile hobbies and pastimes. Only you can decide what is 'worthwhile' and like your bucket list, affordability is an equally key factor. That said many hobbies and pastimes can cost extraordinarily little, save you money in the long term, earn you money, and without a doubt create an enhance state on mind. They might even lengthen your life.

The list is pretty much endless, but here in no particular order are a few to start you thinking:

Gardening and Growing Vegetables

Walking and Rambling

Making Greetings Cards

Home Brewing

Travelling

Tai-Chi or Yoga

Swimming

Tracing Your Ancestry

Cooking and Baking

Fishing

Being Part of a Choir

Cycling

Playing Golf

Arts and Crafts

Learning A Language

Cinema and Theatre Visits

Creative Writing

Photography

Quizzing

Book Clubs

Painting

Knitting and Crochet

Wood Turning

Volunteering and Fundraising

Do it Yourself (DIY) and Home Enhancement

Learning To Play a Musical Instrument

Many of these activities can be done as an individual, but for better all-round mental health it is always good to take part in hobbies and activities as part of a group. The social aspect of taking part in a hobby can be extremely rewarding for several reasons. Even in retirement (like in our working lives) structure is important so it is good to be involved in more than one thing and create a planner for when to take part in hobbies and pastimes.

In your local area you will find many local clubs that offer an immense variety of themes. Many are part of national organisations, and some are just local initiatives such as Men's Sheds etc. Just like the earlier list, here are a few to whet your appetite and get you thinking:

Probus

U3A

Royal British Legion

Women's Institute

Local Photography Clubs

Bridge Groups

Amateur Dramatics

Water Sports Clubs

Masonic Lodges

Royal Voluntary Services

Libraries

Local History Societies

Local Church Groups

Whatever your interests, there will always be something out there for you. Many at no cost to you.

Creating cherished memories, expanding knowledge, the thrill of travelling, or just shear indulgence, holidays during retirement can be made extra special and are not always dictated by having a large budget. Decide on the regularity of when you take your holidays. This may be dictated by either budget or fitting in around your extended family's needs, but ultimately retirement is the time to be a little bit selfish, after all you've earned it.

Where do older people like to travel to?

The list goes on but here are some of the best vacation ideas and destinations for the older generation:

U.S. National Parks. GOOD FOR: adventure, discounts, road trips, multigenerational fun.

The Caribbean. GOOD FOR: relaxation, low physical activity.

Central Europe's Rivers. GOOD FOR: easy pace, low to high activity level.

European City Breaks.

Australia.

Machu Picchu.

Canadian Rockies.

Thailand.

India.

The Canaries.

Whether you are taking time out for that incredibly special holiday of a lifetime, the world is a big place and there is certainly something for everyone. But beware, all holidays come with some problems as we get older, and the rules are constantly changing.

A holiday wherever it is will cost you money, and a budget is the first thing to agree on before starting the planning. You can use a tour operator who will charge you a fee for making your arrangements or you can plan yourself. If opting for the latter, make sure you are meticulous in your planning from airport transfers to insurance, every bit is equally important. Use a *trip planner* to get a personalised day by day itinerary for your *vacation*. There are many on the internet that help you to *plan* your *holiday*.

When compiling your checklist make sure you include and budget for the following (not a definitive list, but a good start):

Realistic and affordable budget.

All flights and transfers.

Airport taxes, not always included in some countries.

Additional baggage fees checked what is and what is not allowed.

Travel insurance, fully inclusive for entire duration, check what is and is not included.

Medical insurance (age and existing ailments checked).

Travel to and from airports / ports.

Suitable clothing for all countries to be visited.

Hire cars and relevant driving licences, do not assume UK licence is acceptable.

Travel visas and passport in date and beyond in case of delays.

Medication for the duration with copy prescriptions (proof might be asked for in some countries.

Details of what hotels etc includes in price, meals, drinks, entertainment etc.

Spending monies and card payment backup, local currency for tips.

Local weather forecasts.

Local travel passes for public transport, venues and tours, some group passes may save money.

As with all stages of life money matters are equally as important when you retire, many will agree that post retirement money matters are to the most important thing as generally money will be less than during you working life. As money will almost certainly be less it is wise to budget, strictly to start with and keep a record to see if the budget needs adjusting. Many people run a household spreadsheet to keep a tally on what is being spent and where there is room for any leeway. A spreadsheet or notebook to record income and expenditure is a sure-fire way of trying to stay within budget.

Savings

Use your saving wisely, Premium Bonds are a safe bet and you have a very small chance to win big. According to UK savings statistics 2022 the average person in the UK has £17,365 in their savings. 34% of adults had either no savings, or less than £1000, in a savings account. 61% of UK adults save money either every, or most, months. 25% of UK adults have less than £100 put away.

Credit

As a newly retired person ask the question – is credit a wise move? The best advice is to only obtain credit that you can afford to pay back quickly. Ideally credit card balances should be settled monthly, so no charges or interest is payable.

If you are looking for a credit loan, approach your bank, they are likely to offer the best and most affordable credit terms. Never use local unregulated lenders or loan sharks as the consequences can be excessive repayments, along with other problems. In the UK almost half of people who use credit are anxious about how much they owe.

Equity Release

A fast-growing way of generating income today is unlocking capital in your property. But beware when considering one of these schemes the lenders value of your property may be much lower than your understanding of the market value.

Ensure you get independent advice before proceeding into an equity release scheme and you will need to employ a solicitor to carry out the legal work. Equity release can take up to 8 weeks to put in place.

Remember that just like a mortgage an equity release attracts compound interest and if you took out £25,000 at 7.5% you would owe £52,000 10 years later. If this was being spent on a dream holiday, then it would be a very expensive holiday in real terms.

What is equity release?

Equity release lets homeowners aged 55 and over release tax-free cash from the value of their home. The amount you can release is based on your age and how much your home is worth. Depending on the equity release product you choose, you can claim your money as one big lump sum or as a series of smaller lump sums.

There are primarily 2 types of equity release;

Lifetime mortgage: you take out a mortgage secured on your property provided it's your main residence, while retaining ownership.

Home reversion: you sell part or all of your home to a home reversion provider in return for a lump sum or regular payments.

Lifetime Mortgage

What is the minimum age you can take out a lifetime mortgage? Usually, it's 55. We're all living longer so the earlier you start the more it's likely to cost in the long run especially if you choose not to pay interest during the term of the lifetime mortgage.

What's the maximum percentage you can borrow? You can borrow a percentage of the value of your property, but this depends on a number of factors; such as your age and the value of your property. The percentage typically increases according to your age when you take out the lifetime mortgage, while some providers might offer larger sums to those with certain past or present medical conditions.

Can the interest rate be fixed? Yes, but if they're variable, there must be a "cap" (upper limit) which won't change for the life of the loan (Equity Release Council standard).

Make sure the product has a 'no negative equity guarantee'. This means when your property is sold, and agents' and solicitors' fees have been paid, even if the amount left is not enough to repay the outstanding loan to your provider, neither you nor your estate will be liable to pay any more (Equity Release Council standard).

Ensure you have the right to move to another property subject to the new property being acceptable to your product provider as continuing security for your equity release loan (Equity Release Council standard). Different lifetime mortgage providers might have slightly different policies.

Whether you can pay none, some or all of the interest. If you can make repayments, it will reduce the total amount of interest payable when the property is sold. With a lifetime mortgage where you can make monthly payments, the amount you can repay might be based on your income. Providers will have to check you can afford these regular payments.

Whether you can withdraw the equity you're releasing in small amounts as and when you need it or whether you have to take it as one lump sum. The advantage of being able to take money out in smaller amounts is you only pay the interest on the amount you've withdrawn. If you can take smaller lump sums, make sure you check if there's a minimum amount.

Home Reversion

Home reversion allows you to sell some or all of your home to a home reversion provider.

The provider effectively co-owns your home, unless you've sold the whole property, but you keep the right to live there for the rest of your life, potentially rent-free.

In return you'll get a lump sum or regular payments.

You'll normally get between 20% and 60% of the market value of your home *(or of the part you sell)*.

When considering a home reversion plan, you should check:

Whether or not you can release equity in several payments or in one lump sum.

The minimum age at which you can take out a home reversion plan.

Some home reversion providers insist you're at least 60 or 65 before you can apply.

The percentage of the market value you will receive. This will increase the older you are when you take out the plan but might vary from provider to provider.

Life Insurance

After your retirement has started I the question always raises – do I really need life insurance? There is no right or wrong answer to this question and it is really down to how well you have planned your retirement.

A well-planned retirement fund and pension along with pre-paid funeral bonds is probably a better plan than paying monthly for Life Insurance. Also, some life insurance policies for the elderly will only pay out if you die before your 90th birthday. So, reading the small print is critical on any life insurance policy taken out in later life.

Investment

There are sensible rules to follow when investing money of any sort and always seek assurances from organisations such as the Financial Conduct Authority FCA. Here are the top 10 rules to follow for all sensible investments:

1. Set yourself goals - Knowing what your financial goals are and what sort of timeframe you are investing over may help you stick to your strategy. eg, if you have long-terms goals, you may be less tempted to dip into your investments before you stop work.

2. The bigger the returns, the bigger the level of risk - The prospect of higher returns may be appealing, but there's usually a greater risk of losing your money. Think carefully about your approach to risk. You may be more comfortable opting for less risky investments, even if returns are likely to be lower. Remember though, that no investment comes without risk, and there is always the chance you could get back less than you put in.

3. Don't put all your eggs in one basket - We all know the saying 'don't put all your eggs in one basket', but it's particularly important to apply this rule when investing. Spreading your money across a range of different types of assets and geographical areas means you won't be depending too heavily on one kind of investment or region. That means if one of them performs badly, hopefully some of your other investments might make up for these losses, although nothing is guaranteed.

4. Invest for the long-term - Investing should never be considered a 'get rich quick' scheme. You need to remain invested for at least five years, but preferably much longer to give your investments the best chance of providing the returns you're hoping for. Even then you must be comfortable accepting the risk that you could get less than you put in. If your investment goals are short-term, for example, two or three years away, investing won't be right for you, as you'll need to keep your money readily accessible, usually in a savings account.

5. If it seems too good to be true, it probably is - Beware highly speculative investments that seem too good to be true, and don't follow the herd and invest just because other people are. For example, many investors piled into digital currency Bitcoin in the latter half of 2017 as its price surged, only to see its value halve in a month.

6. Never invest in anything you don't understand - Before you put your money into any investment, take time to research it thoroughly, so you understand exactly what's involved and what the risks are.

7. Factor in charges - Charges will have an impact on your overall returns, so it's important to take these into consideration when choosing your investments

8. Reinvesting income can help boost overall returns - If you don't need an income from your investments, you may want to consider reinvesting it to buy more of your investment which will potentially grow in value and boost your overall returns.

9. Don't try to time the market - In an ideal world, you'd be able to buy investments just before they increase in value and sell before they fall. However, no-one knows which way stock markets will move next, so trying to predict market ups and downs could mean that you end up buying or selling at just the wrong time.

10. Review your portfolio - Although too much tinkering with your investments isn't usually a good idea, that doesn't mean you should just forget about them. Your investments will change in value over time which may mean your asset allocation – how you choose to split your money between different assets, such as shares, bonds, cash and property – moves out of line with your investment objectives. On occasion it may be wise to use a financial management company to manage your portfolio.

Investment Scams

One of the biggest criminal acts in the world today are investment scams. Many unscrupulous criminal prey on older people as they believe they a more likely to fall for a dodgy investment. Criminals also believe that older people have more money to lose and will not miss it. Be prepared and say no to everything, do your homework and ask for guarantees, and always ask a third party before committing to anything. One of the biggest scams in the marketplace today is 'Crypto Currency'. Many people have lost large amounts of cash in this field.

How do investment scams work?

Scammers use social media and online forums to create fake news and excitement in listed stocks to increase (or 'pump') the share price. Then they sell (or 'dump') their shares and take a profit, leaving the share price to fall. Any other investors are left with low value shares and will lose money.

What are the latest common scams and frauds to look out for?

COVID-19 scams, rumours, and price gouging.

Banking Scams.

Telephone Scams.

Census-Related Fraud.

Government Grant Scams.

Investment Scams.

Crypto Currency.

Whisky and Wine Investments.

Lottery and Sweepstakes Scams.

Charity Scams.

What are the 8 most common scams?

Emergency Scams.

HMR&C or Government Imposter Scams.

Foreign Money Exchange Scams.

Counterfeit Cashier's Checks.

Bogus Debts.

Home Repair Scams, often called Home Improvements.

Business Opportunities or Employment Scams.

Shopping Sprees. You get a phone call, offering you a '£500 shopping spree' (or another amount).

2.1E. Benefits and Government Assistance

Every year, billions of pounds of state benefits go unclaimed. Being familiar with what you are entitled to ensure you are not one of the many that miss out. It is one of life's misconceptions that the Government of your Local Authority will let you know what your entitlements are, let's be totally clear about this – it never happens. In this section we will highlight the benefits that are available, the list is not complete and constantly changes, as does the entitlement. For this reason, it is especially important that you keep yourself up to date with what is available. For most people, you have paid into a welfare system, so now is the time to use it when you need to.

If you are not comfortable finding out what is available speak to charities such as 'AGE UK' who have qualified advisors to help to gain what you are entitled to. The Government Website also gives up to date information relating to all benefits and entitlements. A very good and highly recommended organisation is 'Turn2Us'. Turn2us is a national charity providing practical help to people who are struggling financially. Their website can be found at https://www.turn2us.org.uk/About-Us

Breaking it down these are the types of help out there:

Help to pay bills.

Heating Benefits

Public Transport Concessions

Housing Benefit

TV Licence Concessions

Council Tax Support

Assistance With Urgent or One-Off Expenses

Government Help with Energy Bills

Help to boost income!

Employment and Support Allowance

Pension Credit

Personal Independence Payments

Income Support

Universal Credit

Cost of living payments

Help pay for care or bereavement.

Attendance Allowance

Carer's Allowance

Health Benefits

Bereavement benefits

As stated earlier this list is not definitive and will change from time to time, as do the entitlements, but being familiar with what is out there if often more important, knowledge is king!

2.1F. Children, Grandchildren and Communication

Sometimes a burden, and sometimes a cause for concern; children and grandchildren will offer advice to you on how you should run your life, invest 'their' inheritance and generally look after yourself 'as they see it'. Some advice may be positive and good for you and on occasions the advice may be totally out of order. They will always say it is in your best interest, but is it? Be rational and ask questions in a supportive way; ask questions, is it really the best for me?

Only you can decide on how close or distant you wish to be with your relatives', but it is not always best take everything they say at face value. Most of all it is best to stay connected with your loved ones. At some stage you will need them, so do not burn any bridges and cut off all ties.

At some stage you may be in a position to ask them to look after your affairs, financial, medical and legal through

Powers of Attorney. They may also be the ones that decide on a care home for you.

Having pets in retirement has been questioned by may over the years with claims that they pet is a burden, the person cannot exercise the pet properly, etc. But many studies have been carried out in recent years to promote the benefits of being a pet owner. Pets (especially dogs can encourage a routine for retired people and almost certainly additional exercise.

Is it good for old people to have pets?

Overall pets increase opportunities for exercise and outdoor activities. Pets also contribute to better cognitive function in older adults and provide more opportunities to socialize. Having a pet is also linked to health benefits such as decreased blood pressure, cholesterol levels, and triglyceride levels.

Why do pets help older people live happier and longer?

Many studies suggest that pets can positively influence factors that contribute to longevity, including reducing stress, facilitating resiliency against cardiovascular disease, and connecting us to a network of social support.

Pets and Depression

Some studies have shown that pet owners are far less likely to suffer from depression than older people without pets. People with limited human social supports often experience feelings of loneliness and isolation, both of which can worsen depression. A pet helps to decrease these feelings by providing companionship to its owner.

Dog owners have better results after a major health event.

Recent studies found that, overall, dog owners tend to live longer than non-owners. And they often recover better from major health events such as a heart attack or stroke, especially if they live alone.

A nationally representative survey of pet owners and non-pet owners commissioned by HABRI and Mars Petcare found that: 85% of respondents agree interaction that pets can help reduce loneliness. 76% agree human-pet interactions can help address social isolation.

Overall pet ownership does come down to health and financial commitment. Yes, you do need to have a certain level of mobility for pet ownership and a responsible pet owner will require insurance, visits to the vet, and possibly kennels when away on holiday. For a medium sized dog, the annual costs can exceed £2,000 per year. Remember this when buying or replacing a pet and carry out a realistic cost analysis of what it will cost to keep. Pets are a lifetime (for them) commitment.

Many people who are retired have a wealth of knowledge and experience that can benefit a huge number of organisations in the UK. Many of the skills that we have learnt in our professional lives can benefit both national and local charities. So why not step forward and volunteer. The range of charities is immense and without a doubt they provide something for everyone. You can do as little or as much as you want to, and some will even help will out of pocket expenses.

Local government and lobbying groups can also be a rewarding part time occupation, again putting together your life's experiences, it can benefit your local community. Councillors not only represent their communities and residents, but they also help to make and shape the policies of the council. They do not directly manage services, but they do make the decisions on what those services will be like. Councillors attend various meetings in order to carry out their duties. Councillors do not get paid a salary, however they do receive an annual allowance which reimburses them for time they have spent on council duties, as well as telephone and other office expenses.

Public speaking is the process of communicating information to a live audience. The type of information communicated is deliberately structured to inform, persuade, and entertain. Many people fear they suffer from a public speaking weakness and lack the will to master the skill. Public speaking can benefit local communities and if you are good at it can earn you money as a part time job. It is not unusual to charge between £400 and £1,000 for an evening of public speaking at a private venue.

2.1J. Part Time Work

Why are we covering part time work? It is an area that many retired people enter into whether or not the work is paid or unpaid, many retired people still like to work, but usually on their terms. For many the additional income is great for supplementing their pensions.

The range of work that retirees carry out on a part time basis is pretty much endless. Although there are some favourites that many enter into, for example:

Retail Shop Work

Driving Jobs

Handyman services

Internet Selling such as eBay or Marketplace

Car Boot Sales

Cleaning and Housework

Dog Walking

Gardening

Paid Mystery Shopping – www.mystery-shoppers.co.uk

Freelance Consultancy

And the list goes on, but remember the important factors when considering part time work:

Are you physically fit enough to carry out the work?

Do you need any special licences, medicals or insurance?

You will more than likely have to pay base rate tax on anything you earn.

Not every employer will offer the shifts that you want.

Sometimes a self-employed position is a better consideration.

2.2 Making the Most of the Early Years

2.2A. First Aid and Preventing Accidents

2.2B. Dieting

2.2C. Exercise

2.2D. Bad Habits

2.2E. Blood Donation and Organ Donations

Retirement is all about making the most of the early years. It is inevitable that in later retirement you will suffer from some type of age-related illness. Sadly, we are not immortal, and this will come at some stage. To aid the aging process and to make the most of retirement it is critical to get it right and reduce the aging process wherever possible. This can be done by reducing risks, sensible dieting, a strong exercise regime, dropping some bad habits and a positive mental outlook on life.

What are the keys to aging well?

Get regular exercise.

Be sure to visit the doctor.

Sleep 7 to 9 hours each night.

Keep a positive mindset.

Stay connected to your loved ones.

Learn something new.

Eat a balanced, healthy diet.

Do what you love to do.

2.2A. First Aid and Preventing Accidents

As you may well be spending more time at home, it is wise to be familiar with up to date first aid in the home. Many local community groups offer short courses in this area. Also, it is good to know where a defibrillator is in relation to your home. Armed with this information in might even save your partners or your life.

According to The Royal Society for Preventing Accidents ROSPA.

The home is the most common location for an accident to happen.

Every year across the UK, there are approximately 6,000 deaths because of home accidents.

Children under the age of five years and people in later life (those over the age of 65, and particularly those over 75) are most likely to have an accident at home.

Falls are the most common accidents and can cause serious injury at any time of life, but the risk increases with age.

More women than men over the age of 65 die as a direct result of an accident in the home; however, among children more boys than girls have accidents in the home.

In 2020, 141 pedal cyclists were killed, 4,215 seriously injured and 11,938 slightly injured in Great Britain.

The statistics speak for themselves and being elderly increases the risk of an accident. That said, many accidents can be avoidable by carrying out a mental last minute risk assessment or LMRA. Put simply before any task ask yourself the simple question, what are the risks? what should I do to prevent or reduce the risks? After all you would not cross a busy road without looking to see if it is clear to do so. An LMRA is the same for everything in life. Reduce the risk and reduce the chance of accidents.

2.2B. Dieting

When people reach the grand old age of 100, it rarely happens by chance and diet counts a lot towards surviving well into old age. It has been well publicised that there are many foods that are bad for us, these include the high cholesterol and high sugar foods.

Once anyone has eaten to excess for a few years it becomes difficult to turn the clock back. But in retirement it makes even more sense to concentrate more on a healthy diet. Plenty of fresh produce, smaller portions and trying to cut out processed foods are all the sensible options.

Healthy food supplements and multi vitamins are essential in retirement for better health and improved preservation of the body. They also help to improve the body's immune system for protection against minor illnesses.

Alcohol in moderation is the future for retirement, it has been well documented that alcohol affects the memory, but even more so in elder people. It may seem to be a challenge but try and keep below the recommended 14 units a week.

Drinking too much alcohol can raise blood pressure to unhealthy levels. Having more than three drinks in one sitting temporarily raises blood pressure. Repeated binge drinking can lead to long-term increases in blood pressure, increasing the risk of heart attack.

All alcoholic drinks, including red and white wine, beer, and spirits, are linked with cancer. The more you drink, the higher your cancer risk.

A New genetic study in 2022 confirms that alcohol is a direct cause of cancer. New data from a large-scale genetic study led by Oxford Population Health confirms that alcohol directly causes cancer. Worldwide, alcohol may cause around 3 million deaths each year, including over 400,000 from cancer.

Excessive alcohol consumption over a lengthy period of time, can also lead to brain damage and may increase your risk of developing dementia. However, drinking alcohol in moderation has not been conclusively linked to an increased dementia risk, nor has it been shown to offer significant protection against developing dementia.

2.2C. Exercise

A guaranteed way of staying fit and keeping out of the doctors' waiting room is from regular exercise; walking, swimming, yoga, whatever floats your boat. A steady and regular exercise regime is the future for older people.

Try a mixture of disciplines, and it can be part of your daily routines such as walking the dog. Wild swimming is a fast-growing way of exercising but make sure you do not do it alone for your own personal safety.

Try and create daily or weekly targets; such as 10,000 steps a day or walking 5 miles a day. In harsh weather walk up

and down stairs 20 times. When you have completed your
mini workout, you should be out of breath, if not you may
want to try harder next time.

A handy gadget to have for exercise is a smart watch. There
are many on the market and they can monitor your distance
walk, steps, heart rate and blood pressure.

2.2D. Bad Habits

Turning unhealthy habits around will always be a challenge,
even more so post retirement. During your working life a
busy schedule that prevented a person from engaging in
healthy practices can no longer be used as an excuse.
Negative relationships of obesity, smoking, heavy drinking,
poor diet, and lack of physical activity with morbidity and
mortality have been shown to be deadly and a guaranteed
way of shortening your retirement.

For these reasons it becomes critical to drop the unhealthy
habits when you retire. If you are struggling with this, there is
help out there in the community. Talk to your GP and get
help quickly before it is too late. After all, when you are
retired the excuse, I do not have time can no longer be used.

2.2E. Blood Donation and Organ Donations

A common misconception for the older generation is that you
cannot take part in blood donations and organ donations. In
some respect this may be true. But generally, both types of

donations can carry on if you are in reasonable health. There is no upper age limit for becoming an organ donor. That said, the decision about whether some or all organs or tissue are suitable for transplant is always made at the time my medical specialist at the time of donation, considering your medical, travel and social history. This rule applies whatever the age of the donor.

What are the requirements to donate blood in the UK?

To donate blood, you will need to:

be generally fit and well.

be aged between 17 and 65.

weigh between 7 stone 12 lbs (50kg) and 25 stone (158kg)

have suitable veins (we will check these before you donate)

meet all donor eligibility criteria (we will check this with you before you donate)

In general, if you are fit and healthy, weigh over 7 stone 12 lbs (50kg) and are aged between 17 and 66 (up to 70 if you have given blood before) you should be able to give blood. If you are over 70, you need to have given blood in the last two years to continue donating.

<u>2.3 You and Your Home</u>

2.3A. Accommodation

2.3B. Down-Sizing

2.3C. Park Homes

2.4D. Retirement Homes

2.5E. Emigrating

2.3 You and Your Home

In the UK 65.1% of the UK are homeowners with or without outstanding mortgages or loans. 37.5% of the UK population are homeowners with mortgages or loans. 27.6% of the UK population are homeowners without outstanding mortgages or loans.

Of those in the population aged over 55 about 54% own their own property. *(2022 Figures)* It is fair to assume that those without a mortgage are aged over 55. Presumably, the rest of people either rent, have work provided accommodation or live with relatives.

Having more disposable income, and no interest to pay, are just some of the great benefits to being mortgage free. When you pay off your mortgage, you'll have much more money to put into savings, spend on yourself and access when you need it.

A thoughtful consideration to be made when receiving any redundancy payment of early retirement bonus. There are certainly no tax benefits of keeping a mortgage, so debt free is a wonderful way to start your retirement.

No matter which category you fall into have secure accommodation is exceedingly high on anyone's agenda, and if you are not paying for it in terms of a mortgage or rent, then your retirement will be easier than many.

It also is understood that rent increases and fluctuation in mortgage rates are also a factor that needs to be considered when budgeting.

2.3A. Accommodation

Your accommodation will still be a big investment irrespective of whether you are paying rent or mortgage. Owned out right will still attract maintenance costs, council rates and possible enhancements along the way. Remember that if you are single in any type residence you are entitled a 25% discount of your local council taxes.

2.3B. Down-Sizing

The word 'Down-Sizing' is used a lot when heading towards retirement. Down-Sizing is the sale of the family home for a property that is generally smaller cheaper to run and more manageable. Many people move elsewhere in the country into a new community just prior to retirement, and in a property more suited to retirement.

2.3C. Park Homes

Following a decision to down-size a Park Home is sometimes a consideration. But like everything involving large sums of money, do your homework before deciding. Something that looks like a bargain invariably never is. The following questions are all critical to making your decision.

Is it worth buying a park home UK?

But, ultimately, it's up to you to decide whether a park home is a good investment. (Many would say they are not an investment, akin to buying a car) They're affordable, easy to maintain, secure, and make way for modern living in a tight-knit community. But they can lose value quickly, and you may find yourself stuck with extra costs, such as ground rent and commission fees. The rent quite often increases well above inflation, making them unaffordable in the long term.

What are the pitfalls of buying a park home UK?

The cons of park home living: It is extremely unlikely that they will increase in value over time. You can't get a mortgage on a park home. They require regular maintenance. Occasionally they are high in energy costs. It has been reported that on some Park Home sites, mail and deliveries can only be made to receptions and not to your door.

Do you need a solicitor to buy a park home?

Legally there is no requirement to instruct a Solicitor when buying a park home, however, by not doing so means taking a huge risk. It is very common to see how quickly a park home purchase can go wrong, especially if the site owner is not above dodgy tactics to secure revenue. Sadly, it is generally after monies have exchanged hands.

2.3D. Retirement Homes

The property market now has a large number of new retirement homes being added to the market. Well-known companies such as 'Churchill Retirement https://www.churchillretirement.co.uk/ and McCarthy Stone https://www.mccarthyandstone.co.uk/ are continuing to bring high quality flats to the marketplace. These properties and purpose built and built to a high standard. They also have ready-made communal rooms within the developments.

However, they are expensive and do come with a service charge that includes grounds maintenance and on site management, sometimes including security. These properties and generally leasehold and occasionally available to rent. It has been said that the rules imposed on the residents in these types of developments are sometimes extreme, but the rules are set to benefit all of the community within the development.

What to consider before you buy into a retirement village?

The purchase price. One of the biggest downsides is cost, they tend to be overpriced.

Service charges and ground rent; are they fixed? If so for how long?

What is the resale value?

Failure to accommodate your specific health needs.

Quite often, no changes can be made to décor etc.

Are there any exit fees if you sell?

2.3E. Emigrating

Many people have the dream to retire into the sun but is it all that it is cracked up to be. Some of advantages include:

Getting a better place to live,

Interacting with people and learning their way of live.

Possibly better weather and a cheaper way of living.

For all of these reason emigration can be seen as a positive consideration for retirees.

On the negative side, Health is obviously a main concern, and you will almost certainly need private medical insurance. Being some distance from loved ones is also a concern for many. Since the UK left the EU some countries are insisting that members of the British community prove they have sufficient income to live in their country and some are insisting on changing your nationality, or having a permanent visa to live in the country.

Accommodation and local taxes may differ greatly from the UK. Learning the local language is also a must if you are to fully integrate into the community.

What happens to my UK pension if I emigrate?

You can claim and receive a UK State Pension while living overseas. But Pension Credit stops when you move overseas permanently.

Pension credit is a means-tested benefit, which can top up your weekly income. Your State Pension can be paid to a UK bank or building society account, or to an overseas account in the local currency, the choice is yours.

You will also have to factor in exchange rates into local currency. You can get pension increases yearly if you live in a European Economic Area (EEA) country or a country which has a social security agreement with the UK, but this is not guaranteed in every country.

2.4A. The Internet

2.4B. Streaming and Podcasts

2.4C. Social Media

2.4D. Artificial Intelligence

2.4E. Online Scams

2.4F. Technology Aids and Digital Home Assistants

This book has no wish to assume that all retired people are not familiar with modern technology. In fact, the majority are remarkably familiar with the technology out there. If you feel you need help, then read on, alternatively skip this section entirely. It would be wrong to miss out this section from the book as it may benefit some readers.

The elder population has on many occasions been criticised for not moving with the times and embracing modern technology. In many areas this may be true, but things are changing fast, and the elder generation are now becoming more internet savvy and through their recent experiences in the workplace have fully understood modern technology.

To survive in the modern world, it has now become critical to have a full understanding in modern technology as well as keeping up to date with changes. Having internet in your home is now as common as having a telephone or a television, and with the fast-changing world an internet connection has become an essential part of modern living.

Many courses are available locally and the fallback is asking the grandchildren who now tend to learn 'IT' before they can walk. For those not familiar with the modern technology terminology the following are brief explanations:

2.4A. The Internet

Invented in 1983 and made public some 10 years later, the Internet, sometimes called simply "the Net," is a worldwide system of computer networks - a network of networks in which users at any one computer can, if they have permission, get information from any other computer (and sometimes talk directly to users at other computers).

In the early days, the internet was not highly effective as computers and devices were not powerful enough to use it to its full potential. In recent years, the power of the internet is at everyone's fingertips, and the internet governs much of the way we interact as a human race.

2.4B. Streaming and Podcasts

The word streaming is used frequently in daily life, and days of watching VHS cassettes and DVD Films are coming to an end. Streaming films or programs on a digital television connected to the internet are fast becoming the norm.

What is streaming and how does it work?

The term streaming refers to the continual transmission of audio and video files from a server to a client. In video streams, content is sent in a compressed form over the internet and is displayed by the viewer in real time.

The media is sent in a continuous stream of data and is played as it arrives.

Many television channels are switching to online versions, and it can be assumed that in time, this will eventually replace all terrestrial broadcasting.

Streaming can also apply to music and podcasts as well as just video images.

What is a podcast and how does it work?

Podcasting is the preparation and distribution of audio files using RSS feeds *(Really Simple Syndication)* to the computers of subscribed users. These files may then be uploaded to streaming services, which users can listen to on their smartphones or digital music and multimedia players, like an iPod. Some people look at them as a modern-day newspaper and normally come in episodes. There are over 3 million podcasts on the internet as at 2022.

2.4C. Social Media

Social Media are websites and applications that enable users to create and share content or to take part in social networking. They come in a variety of formats with 'Facebook', 'Twitter', 'Instagram' and 'Linked In' being the main ones. Whether or not you use social media is a personal choice, however it is a good form of communication to keep engaged with social groups during retirement. On the negative side it does have an amount of misinformation posted on its pages, which on occasions can cloud judgement and be misleading.

Artificial Intelligence often referred to as 'AI' is the theory and development of computer systems able to perform tasks normally requiring human intelligence, such as visual perception, speech recognition, decision-making, and translation between languages. Many devices use AI as part of their generic operating systems. For the retired generation AI can be immensely helpful in day-to-day planning. At its simplest form, artificial intelligence is a field, which combines computer science and robust datasets, to enable problem-solving.

Online scams, also known as internet scams, continue to evolve and can vary widely.

The term generally refers to someone using internet services or software to defraud or take advantage of victims, typically for financial gain. Sadly, the elderly and the retired population are considered fair game to scammers.

For this reason, it is critical to be extra vigilant in anything remotely suspicious or unusual. The Golden Rule is if it sounds to be good to be true – then quite simply it is!

What Are Internet Scams?

Internet scams are different methodologies of Fraud, eased by cybercriminals on the Internet. Frauds or Scams can happen in a myriad of ways- via phishing emails, social media, SMS or Text messages on your mobile phone, fake tech support phone calls, scareware and more.

These types of scams can range from credit card theft, capturing user login and password credentials and even identity theft.

Most Common Types of Online Scams?

Phishing

The top online scam today is Phishing. Internet thieves' prey on unsuspecting users by sending out phishing emails.

In these emails, a cybercriminal tries to trick you into believing you are logging into a trusted website that you normally do business with. This could be a bank, your social media account, an online shopping website, shipping companies, cloud storage companies and more.

Another type of popular phishing scam is the Nigerian Prince, or 419 scam. These are phishing emails in which you're asked to help bring large sums of money into the country, cash phony money orders or wire money to the thief.

The trick is that the scammer first asks you for a small fee because the larger sum of money is "tied up" whether it be in wire transfer fees, processing fees or some other tall tale.

Fake AV (anti-virus)

One close to our industry is fake security software, which is also known as scareware. These start with a pop-up warning saying that you have a virus. Then the popup leads the user to believe that if they click on the link, the infection will get cleaned up. Cybercriminals use the promise of "Free Anti-Virus" to instead implant malware on a victim's device.

Social Media Scams

Social media scams are a variety of posts you will see in your news feeds- all with the goal of getting you to click on a link that could potentially be hosting malware.

Mobile Scams

Mobile scams can come in many forms, but the most common are phishing apps. These apps are designed to look like the real thing, just like phishing emails. It is the same premise, however, instead of emails, the malware is passed through a fake app.

Social Engineering Scams

Social engineering is a way that cybercriminals use human-to-human interaction in order to get the user to divulge sensitive information. Since social engineering is based on human nature and emotional reactions, there are many ways that attackers can try to trick you- online and offline.

2.4F. Technology Aids and Digital Home Assistants

In recent years the technology sector has mover at an alarming pace, with numerous gadgets and software packages that really help the retired and aging population. For example, electronic home assistants can carry out a multitude of tasks to assist you in your daily life, as well as being very simple to use.

What is a Digital Home Assistant?

A digital home assistant is an electronic device which responds to voice commands to do things for you such as answer questions and control networked home appliances. Using your home Internet network, the digital home assistant can adjust lights, heat, garage doors, play music, and search the Internet.

There are many home assistants on the market that carry out a variety of tasks, for example:

Diary Management

Video Telephone Calls

Playing Music and Podcasts

Managing Photographs and Photo Albums

Managing Home Automation such as switching of and off lights and heating.

Streaming Films.

Creating Shopping Lists and Reminders.

It would be wrong to say which is the best_digital home assistant on the market as the marketplace is constantly changing. At the time of writing many consider that 'Amazon Alexa' has the market edge. The Alexa offers the following functionality:

Alexa can show you even more: 8" HD touchscreen, adaptive colour and stereo speakers bring entertainment to life. Make video calls with a 13 MP camera that uses auto-framing to keep you centred.

Stay in frame: make video calls with a new camera that frames and centres automatically. Simply ask Alexa to call your contacts.

Make life easier at home: glance at your calendars and reminders. Use your voice to set timers, update lists, and see news or traffic updates.

Manage your smart home: look in when you're away with the built-in camera. Control compatible devices like cameras, lights and more using the interactive display or your voice.

Be entertained: enjoy TV programmes and films in HD and stereo with Prime Video, Netflix and more. Ask Alexa to stream Amazon Music, Apple Music or Spotify.

Put your memories on display: use Amazon Photos to turn
your home screen into a digital frame. Adaptive colour helps
your favourite photos look great in any light.

Designed to protect your privacy: electronically disconnect
the microphones and camera with the press of a button.
Slide the built-in cover to close the camera.

Podcast have also changed the way we listen to
entertainment. A podcast is an edited piece of content which
can be a complete radio programme, an edited extract or
highlights from a programme, or completely unique content
with a particular theme made to be subscribed and listened
to as a series.

Not every radio programme is available as a podcast. A
podcast can have many purposes, but the main one is to
entertain its audience. Podcast listeners might have one of
several reasons to subscribe to a podcast, such as to: Hear
updates and breakdowns of current events. Learn about a
new topic or industry.

<u>2.5 Physical Health and State of Mind</u>

As the population now lives longer than the much talked about three score years and ten (70), it has now become critical to support good physical and mental health. Not only will this help to avoid unnecessary suffering, but it will also help you to enjoy life and not be a total burden on health services.

It is important to firstly understand the terminology and what it means as well as spotting tell-tale signs with you partner family or peer group.

<u>2.5A. Age Related Medical Conditions</u>

Common health conditions associated with ageing and old age include hearing loss, cataracts, and refractive errors, back and neck pain and osteoarthritis, chronic obstructive pulmonary disease, diabetes, depression and dementia.

The list sadly goes on and on as there are many other diseases that older people are susceptible to. But it is not all doom and gloom, many of these illnesses can be held off with a combination of a good exercise regime, a sensible diet and some health supplements. A good simple guide to health supplements are:

Vitamin A – Helping immunity, skin repair, assists in vision.

Vitamin B - Supports healthy blood, bones, brain, immune system, and the body's ability to use energy.

Vitamin C - Helping to protect against free radical damage and strengthen the immune system.

Vitamin D - Older people need to have enough vitamin D in their diet to maintain their bone health and prevent damage to their bones or muscles when they fall.

Cod Liver Oil - Omega-3 fatty acids are beneficial for seniors who live with respiratory problems such as asthma or COPD. This nutrient can loosen up the airways that normally constrict due to these conditions. Omega-3s also make it easier for seniors to breathe after engaging in moderate exercise or physical therapy.

Good health food shops can advise you on all food supplements that benefit the elderly.

Some however are considered to be hereditary, which sadly cannot be changed. It is therefore important that you are aware of illnesses and diseases that run in your family and steps that can be put in place to slow down any symptoms of those diseases.

What are the 10 most common chronic diseases in older adults?

While this is by no means a comprehensive list of ailments experienced by older adults, these and other chronic diseases are among the more common (*top 10 at the time of writing*):

Arthritis.

Cancer.

Chronic Kidney Disease.

Chronic Obstructive Pulmonary Disease.

Dementia, Alzheimer's, and Parkinson's.

Diabetes.

Osteoporosis.

Heart Attack.

Stroke.

It would be wrong in this book to give medical advice on any of these diseases, your GP or Medical Centre is in a better position to advise on exact symptoms test criteria etc.

With good preventative controls, drugs, and therapies many of these diseases can be slowed down – but only if they have been diagnosed correctly by the relevant experts. Self-diagnosis is not always the best solution.

2.5B. Obesity, The Harsh Truth

The next section is written to advise and not be judgemental, but this book would not be complete without the information on this subject being added, and we have to consider the bigger picture. We understand that unlike addictions to drugs, alcohol, smoking, gambling etc., and addiction to food is different and everyone needs food to live. Obesity is a much bigger and complex issue then the average person can fathom out, and everything in this section is rightly or wrongly generalising the subject. For that reason alone, we apologise in advance if it offends anyone, and we are not setting out to stereotype anyone. We are just telling it the way it is in actual facts.

A sad fact of life in the UK is the amount of Obesity. It is and has been reported as being a problem for over 20 years, but still the problem grows.

As we reach retirement the problem only gets worse with alarmingly large amounts of elderly people being categorised as Obese.

So, what is Obesity?

According to the World Health Organisation (WHO) Overweight and obesity are defined as abnormal or excessive fat accumulation that presents a risk to health. A body mass index (BMI) over 25 is considered overweight, and over 30 is obese. A BMI is calculated by height and total weight only. Obesity is responsible for many of the chronic illnesses that affect older people, in particular Diabetes and **Heart Attack.**

What causes obesity & overweight?

Food and Activity. People gain weight when they eat more calories than they burn through activity.

Environment. The world around us influences our ability to maintain a healthy weight.

Genetics.

Health Conditions and Medications.

Stress, Emotional Factors, and Poor Sleep.

What are the Categories of Obesity?

Obesity and overweight and defined purely by Body Mass Index (BMI). You can check your BMI quite easily by using the internet, smart phone apps, or by visiting your GP.

The categories ad broken into the following:

Normal health weight - BMI below 25

Overweight – BMI over 25

Obese – BMI over 30

Morbidly Obese – BMI over 40

Not surprisingly being morbidly obese sets a huge strain on the body and puts you at risk of numerous ailments. Just being obese can put you in the at-risk category of developing Type 2 Diabetes, a common condition that causes the level of sugar (glucose) in the blood to become too high.

The alarming truth is that in older people are more likely to be overweight. In 2021 people aged 45-74 were more likely to be overweight or obese than any other age groups. 31% of those aged 65-74 years and 24% of those aged 75+ are living with obesity and severe obesity. For the 65-74 age group, prevalence is higher than the 27% average of obesity and severe obesity seen across all age groups.

The good news is that it is not tool late when you are retired, and many can turn the clock back achieving a healthy weight, by following a sensible diet and a simple exercise regime.

2.5C. Exercise Regimes

An exercise regime is a set of rules about food, exercise, or even beauty that some people follow to stay healthy or attractive. Swimming, Walking, Yoga, etc.,

Swimming

Swimming makes your heart stronger, larger and improves your cardiovascular health and endurance. It will also lower your blood pressure, improve your circulation and help reduce the risk of heart and lung disease.

Many local health clubs and local authorities run swimming classes, as well as aqua aerobics and other water related exercise.

What are 10 health benefits of swimming?

Swimming Improves Social Well Being.

Swimming Teaches Goal Orientation.

Swimming Makes You Smarter.

Swimming Teaches Team-Building Skills.

Swimming Burns More Calories than Jogging.

Swimming Slows Down Aging.

Swimming is Good for Asthma.

In terms of age markers like muscle mass and lung function swimming really does help you stay younger for longer. A long-term study at Indiana University Centre for the Science of Swimming found that swimmers aged over 35 swimming roughly 3,200 to 4,500 metres three to five times a week, postponed the ageing process.

Walking

Walk to work or to the shops 1-2 times per week or take public transport part of the way and walk the rest.

Take a 10–15-minute brisk walk during your breaks.

Take a 10–15-minute brisk walk before or after meals.

Walk up and down stairs; avoid taking the elevators and escalators.

Walking 'Step by Step' It is strongly recommended that you check with your GP before starting a regular exercise program to ensure you do not have any underlying health issues. Start small an aim big, for example:

Beginner

Try walking briskly at a 3 to 3.5-mph pace (walking a mile in 17-20 minutes), beginning with 10 minutes per day for the first three weeks. Slowly increase the time you walk by 5 minutes per week until you are able to walk 30 minutes per day, six days per week.

Intermediate

 If you are already in good shape, start at this level. If not, you can continue here after about a month of the "Beginner" program. Aiming for a pace of 3.5 to 4.5 mph (13-17 minutes per mile), walk 3 miles (about 45 minutes), 3-5 times per week. If you find that you can't walk that fast, increase the distance that you walk instead.

Advanced

 If you already do fitness walking and/or are in excellent shape, increase the intensity of your workout by doing the following:

Walk/hike with a 10-15 lb. backpack.

Add uphill/downhill and stairclimbing to your regular walks.

Walk on the beach; the sand will increase your intensity level.

Use 2-3 lb hand weights and continue your arm swing motion.

Try racewalking (5-9 mph). There are many local organisations and competitions you can join.

Yoga

A regular yoga exercise routine can improve your quality of life and help you support your independence. However, many older adults struggle to find a safe, low-impact exercise that fits within their fitness levels.

Yoga is an exercise you can do all your life. It's low-impact nature makes it suitable for those with joint pain, osteoporosis, or limited mobility.

Plus, yoga poses can easily be changed to fit your comfort level and physical ability, making it a wonderful exercise for any age group. Studies show that yoga helps your physical, mental, and emotional health. These widespread benefits are particularly valuable as you age.

The benefits of chair yoga for older adults includes loosening and stretching painful muscles, reducing chronic pain, decreasing stress, and improving circulation.

It also reduces anxiety, helps lower blood pressure, protects joints, and builds strength and balance.

Whatever exercise regime you choose or even a mixture of all three, set targets and pick something that you enjoy, or you can do with a partner. This will make the exercise become a more worthwhile activity.

It is good to understand what the terms 'Mental Health', 'Stress', 'Anger' and 'Anxiety' actually mean. They are words used continuously in modern day life, but many of us do not really understand what they mean and how the link into to retirement.

Turning the clock back only 30 years, it was considered that mental health was an unsocial thing and subsequently people did not talk about their personal mental health issues.

It was always considered to be a subject that people just had to shut up and put up with. In recent years, the tide has turned, and it has been proven to be better for mental health issues if everyone to talks about them, the old adage of a problem shared is a problem halved. The bottom line is it is a very personal thing, but ultimately talking about your issues is best.

What is Mental Health?

The World Health Organisation (WHO) defines mental health as 'a state of wellbeing in which the individual realises his or her abilities, can cope with the normal stresses of life, work productively and fruitfully, and is able to make a contribution to his or her community'.

What is stress?

Stress is the body's reaction to feeling threatened or under pressure. It's quite common, can be motivating to help us achieve things in our daily life, and can help us meet the demands of home, work and family life. But too much stress can affect our mood, our body and our relationships – especially when it feels out of our control. It can make us feel anxious and irritable and affect our self-esteem.

Many things can cause stress. You might feel stressed because of one big event or situation in your life. Or it might be a build-up of lots of smaller things. This might make it harder for you to find what's making you feel stressed, or to explain it to other people.

You may experience stress if you:

Feel under lots of pressure.

Face momentous changes in your life

Are worried about something.

Don't have much or any control over the outcome of a situation.

Have responsibilities that you find overwhelming.

Don't have enough work, activities or change in your life.

Experience discrimination, hate or abuse.

Are going through a period of uncertainty.

 Experiencing a lot of stress over a prolonged period can also lead to a feeling of physical, mental and emotional exhaustion, often called burnout.

What is anger?

Anger is an immediate response that arises when we feel threatened or mistreated. Threats can come in many forms and are not just physical. A good example would be falling out over something trivial with a neighbour, like a boundary dispute. If this is not resolved quickly and amicably it grow into long term anger. Feelings of anger arise due to how we interpret and react to certain situations. Everyone has their own triggers for what makes them angry, but some common ones include situations in which we feel: threatened or attacked. frustrated or powerless.

What is anxiety?

Anxiety is a feeling of unease, such as worry or fear, that can be mild or severe. Everyone has feelings of anxiety at some point in their life. Difficult experiences in childhood, adolescence or adulthood are a common trigger for anxiety problems.

Going through stress and trauma when you're noticeably young is likely to have a particularly enormous impact. Experiences which can trigger anxiety problems include things like physical or emotional abuse. As we get older the impact of anxiety increases, possibly because we find ourselves having less control of our own destinies.

Common anxiety signs and symptoms include:

Feeling nervous, restless or tense.

Having a sense of impending danger, panic or doom.

Having an increased heart rate.

Breathing rapidly (hyperventilation)

Sweating.

Trembling.

Feeling weak or tired.

Trouble concentrating or thinking about anything other than the present worry.

Having identified and understood what the terms mean, it is clear to see how they can relate to all of us at some time in our lives. In retirement the terms Mental Health, Stress, Anger and Anxiety can be bought on suddenly by many triggers. During our working lives we normally have coping mechanisms to deal with these issues.

But as a retired person with less to do, sometimes the mind will focus more on deeper thoughts thereby enhancing personal stress, anger and anxiety. It is important for good all-round mental health that help is looked for when these situations arise, and not hope they will just go away.

A good GP will prescribe drugs to help or refer you for other therapy, such as community workshops etc. where people exchange their own experiences and talk about common issues.

What are the signs and symptoms of dementia?

Signs and symptoms of dementia result when once-healthy neurons, or nerve cells, in the brain stop working, lose connections with other brain cells, and die. While everyone loses some neurons as they age, people with dementia experience far greater loss.

The symptoms of dementia can vary and may include:

Experiencing memory loss, poor judgment, and confusion

Difficulty speaking, understanding, and expressing thoughts, or reading and writing.

Shortened attention span, difficulty in holding a conversation.

Wandering and getting lost in a familiar neighbourhood.

Trouble handling money responsibly and paying bills.

Repeating questions

Using unusual words to refer to familiar objects.

Taking longer to complete normal daily tasks.

Losing interest in normal daily activities or events

Hallucinating or experiencing delusions or paranoia

Acting impulsively

Not caring about other people's feelings

Losing balance and problems with movement

A person may need more help with day-to-day living during these late stages of Dementia. Whilst they can probably still take care of other personal needs on their own (such as using the toilet). They could find it difficult to dress appropriately or be unable to remember simple facts about themselves, such as their address or phone number.

However, they usually recognise family and friends and can recall events from years ago (especially their childhood) with great clarity.

There is currently no cure for Dementia, however many trials are underway, and at some time in the future a cure may be found. It is believed that prevention is better than a cure and some actions can be taken to prevent the onset of Dementia; for example, keeping active, reducing alcohol intake, supporting a good diet and keeping social interaction with other people. None of these actions guarantee not developing dementia but trying to follow the guidance is a good start.

A good guide in living with dementia has some simple rules to follow:

Agree – never argue!

Divert – never reason!

Distract – never shame!

Reassure – never lecture!

Reminisce – never say "remember"!

Repeat – never say "I told you"!

Do what they can do - never say "you can't"!

Ask – never demand!

Encourage – never condescend!

Reinforce – never force!

These simple rules will make living with dementia easier to understand and easier for all parties involved.

What are the signs and symptoms of Parkinson's Disease?

Parkinson's disease is a progressive disorder that affects the nervous system and the parts of the body controlled by the nerves. Symptoms start slowly. The first symptom may be a barely noticeable tremor in just one hand. Tremors are common, but the disorder may also cause stiffness or slowing of movement.

In the early stages of Parkinson's disease, your face may show little or no expression. Your arms may not swing when you walk. Your speech may become soft or slurred. Parkinson's disease symptoms worsen as your condition progresses over time.

Although Parkinson's disease can't be cured, medications might significantly improve your symptoms. Occasionally, your health care provider may suggest surgery to regulate certain regions of your brain and improve your symptoms.

Parkinson's disease signs and symptoms can be different for everyone. Early signs may be mild and go unnoticed. Symptoms often begin on one side of the body and usually remain worse on that side, even after symptoms begin to affect the limbs on both sides.

Parkinson's signs and symptoms may include:

Tremor. A tremor, or rhythmic shaking, usually begins in a limb, often your hand or fingers. You may rub your thumb and forefinger back and forth. This is known as a pill-rolling tremor. Your hand may tremble when it's at rest. The shaking may decrease when you are performing tasks.

Slowed movement (bradykinesia). Over time, Parkinson's disease may slow your movement, making simple tasks difficult and time-consuming. Your steps may become shorter when you walk. It may be difficult to get out of a chair. You may drag or shuffle your feet as you try to walk.

Rigid muscles. Muscle stiffness may occur in any part of your body. The stiff muscles can be painful and limit your range of motion.

Impaired posture and balance. Your posture may become stooped. Or you may fall or have balance problems because of Parkinson's disease.

Loss of automatic movements. You may have a decreased ability to perform unconscious movements, including blinking, smiling or swinging your arms when you walk.

Speech changes. You may speak softly, quickly, slur or hesitate before talking. Your speech may be more of a monotone rather than have the usual speech patterns.

Writing changes. It may become hard to write, and your writing may appear small.

At the time of drafting this book there are no immediate cures for Parkinson's Disease, however some trials are currently underway to find a cure or slow down the onset of the disease.

2.5F. Loneliness & Depression

Many people become socially isolated for a variety of reasons, such as getting older or weaker, no longer being the hub of their family, leaving the workplace, the deaths of spouses and friends, or through disability or illness.

This will inevitably cause loneliness and ultimately depression. The figures for people falling into this category is huge. According to Age UK, more than 2 million people in England over the age of 75 live alone, and more than a million older people say they go over a month without speaking to a friend, neighbour or family member.

A report from the National Academies of Sciences, Engineering, and Medicine (NASEM) points out that more than one-third of adults aged 45 and older feel lonely, and nearly one-fourth of adults aged 65 and older are socially isolated. Reasons for living alone include being widowed or never married, having conflict with family members, and negative experiences with earlier roommates.

The authors however also note that despite the varied circumstances that caused older adults to live alone, many also mentioned independence and a sense of freedom.

When planning your retirement, it has become critical that measures are put in place to stop you falling into this category. Becoming a recluse as not good for your long-term mental health. Humans' are socially interactive and therefore getting out and meeting people when you are retired is critical for your own good health.

2.5H. Early Diagnosis to Illness

In the medical world early diagnosis to a medical condition is critical to the curing process. It can be argued that not all illnesses can be cured, but the earlier the condition is diagnosed the better it will be for the person suffering.

The human body is very good at giving tell-tale signs when all is not right. It may seem obvious, but if you are normally well and you have sickness and headaches for 2 or more days, then you should be seeking help. Ignoring a problem will not make it go away.

So, for your piece of mind and possibly your partners, seek medical attention either through NHS111 or your GP, as an early diagnosis could possibly save your life.

Early diagnosis is key to our survival efforts – it means an increased range of treatment options, improved long-term survival and improved quality of life. In the NHS, there are a range of interventions designed to help, but in general through early diagnosis.

Early diagnosis can also help people to plan ahead while they are still able to make important decisions on their care and support needs and on financial and legal matters. It also helps them and their families to receive practical information, advice and guidance to live.

2.6 Mobility & Home Aids

2.6A. Driving Licence

2.6B. Personal Mobility

2.6C. Government Assistance

2.6D. Aids to Living Safely at Home

As we get older it is fair to say that many will need help with personal mobility and aids to help us around the home. Also, some rules will change and although it may seem like an infringement of our personal freedoms, the rules are put in place to protect you and the public. Ignorance of these rules is not a valid excuse in court.

2.6A. Driving Licences

It may be common knowledge that everyone's driving licence expires every 10 years, but not everyone is aware that irrespective of the length of time you have held a driving licence, it also expires at the age of 70. Following this age, the licence will only be valid for 3 years.

For this reason, it is critical to apply for a new driving licence 90 days before you reach your 70th birthday. It is a very good idea to have a medical check before renewing your licence when you reach 70 years of age, and again each time your licence is renewed.

Your application may take longer than usual if it needs to be referred to a doctor. So, allow plenty of time. You can usually keep driving while DVLA are considering your application.

There are also what are known as notifiable medical conditions that will require you to surrender your driving licence. If you continue to drive with a notifiable medical condition being diagnosed, it is also likely that you could be prosecuted and almost certainly you will not be covered by your vehicle insurance.

This list does change periodically so it is best to check with your doctor of the government website for an accurate list. Go to www.gov.uk/health-conditions-and-driving the bottom line is if you are unsure do nor drive. It is estimated that some 900,000 people drive with an expired driving licence, although how many of these are over 70 is not a published figure.

If your licence has expired more than 2 years before re-applying, then your will be expected to retake your driving test.

Failing to follow these simple rules will mean that will be driving illegally and can face a fine of £1,000 and possibly have your vehicle taken away.

2.6B. Mobility Scooters

The marketplace is now full, with a vast selection of Mobility Scooters and electric wheelchairs, and it is not always the disabled that use them. It can be a cheap source of local transport with a reasonable range. Like everything the range available is always dictated by budget, and an entry level mobility scooter can be purchased for as little as £750.

Like making any purchase, do your homework and see what is out there. Make sure you consider the battery size, range on maintenance cost. It is also a prudent step to consider insurance, although not needed by law, it is good for peace of mind in case you have an accident.

2.6C. Personal Mobility

The personal mobility industry in the UK is huge as is the choice of assistance available. We have already covered mobility scooters, but for those who want something less expensive, wheeled walking frames, sticks etc are always a consideration. Check with your local Age UK charity. Many local charities give personal mobility aids away at no cost, occasionally they may ask for a small donation. So definitely worth a look.

2.6D. Government Assistance

Prior to retirement, if you feel you may need some financial help it is worth looking at benefits such as Personal Independence Payments (known as PIP).

What is PIP?

Personal Independence Payment (PIP) is extra money to help you with everyday life if you've an illness, disability or mental health condition. You can get it on top of Employment and Support Allowance or other benefits.

Your income, savings, and whether you're working or not do not affect your eligibility.

These carry on after you have retired but cannot be awarded after you have retired. So, it is worthwhile checking your entitlement a couple of years prior to retirement. If the higher mobility allowance is awarded it can be used to help supply a mobility car.

Always check the Government website for up-to-date rules on PIP as they do change periodically, so make sure you are aware of what you are entitled too. It is understood that you or your partner will require a valid driving licence to drive a mobility car.

Mobility Cars

How can I get a free mobility car?

You can get a Motability car or vehicle if you've been awarded:

The higher rate mobility part of Disability Living Allowance (DLA)

The enhanced rate mobility part of Personal Independence Payment (PIP)

Armed Forces Independence Payment (AFIP) or War Pensioners' Mobility Supplement.

Is it worth getting a car on mobility?

'Motability' regularly benchmark themselves against commercial contract hire and leasing companies. Their size, operational efficiencies and the VAT concession means they are around 43-45% cheaper overall when compared to alternative car leasing company prices.

Generally, the mobility car will have a service package included.

2.6E. Aids to Living Safely at Home

Like many things in modern life the market is full of aids to help us live safer and more comfortably at home. Some could be considered a godsend, but others are just gimmicks. It is safe to say there is probably something for everyone and every condition.

Many items can be sourced from your local medical centre / GPs Surgery, and there are also many community charities that can lend equipment. In addition to this a few specialist healthcare providers are around who can provide (normally on a hire basis) the bigger equipment such as hospital beds hoists for beds, baths etc.

Before you go out and spend a small fortune on equipment ask advice as to what is available free of charge. Typical equipment available are:

Walking frames, rollators and walking sticks.

Wheelchairs.

Raised toilet seats and toilet aids.

Grab handles and support rails for walls.

Bed Pans & Personal Care.

Commodes.

Portable Bidets, Wipers & Accessories.

Electric beds.

External Alarm Call Systems

In this modern world it is not necessary to suffer in silence. There are people and purposeful organisations there to make your life easier and safer.

2.7 Legal Affairs and Family Concerns

2.7A. Wills

2.7B. Living Wills

2.7C. Legacy Wills

2.7D. Probate

2.7E. Cohabiting Couples

2.7F. Same Sex Couples

2.7G. Civil Partnerships

2.7H. Lasting Powers of Attorney

2.7J. Property Trusts

2.7K. The Black Box

2.7A. Wills

A will is a legal document that sets forth your wishes regarding the distribution of your property and the care of any minor children. If you die without a will, those wishes may not be carried out. Further, your heirs may end up spending added time, money, and emotional energy to settle your affairs after you're gone.

Though no single document will likely resolve every issue that arises after your death, a will—officially known as a last will and testament can come close. Here's what you need to know about these vital documents.

Why You Should Have a Will

Some people think that only the very wealthy or those with complicated assets need wills. However, there are many good reasons to have a will.

You can be clear about who gets your assets. You can decide who gets what and how much.

You can keep your assets out of the hands of people you don't want to have them (like an estranged relative).

You can identify who should care for your children. Without a will, the courts will decide.

Your heirs will have a faster and easier time getting access to your assets.

You can plan to save your estate money on taxes. You can also give gifts and charitable donations, which can help offset the estate tax.

What Does a Will Cover?

A will allows you to direct how your belongings; such as bank balances, property, or prized possessions to be distributed. If you have a business or investments, your will can specify who will receive those assets and when.

A will also allow you to direct assets to a charity (or charities) of your choice. Similarly, if you wish to leave assets to an institution or an organization, a will can assure that your wishes are carried out.

While wills generally address the bulk of your assets, some aren't covered by their instructions. Those omissions include pay-outs from the testator's life insurance policy. Since the policy has specified beneficiaries, those individuals will receive the proceeds. The same will likely apply for any investment accounts that are designated as "transfer on death."

Key Takeaways

A will is a document that contains your direct wishes for your property and assets, as well as the care of your dependents.

Failure to prepare a will typically leave decisions about your estate in the hands of judges or state officials and may also cause family strife.

You can prepare a valid will yourself, but you should have the document witnessed to decrease the likelihood of successful challenges later.

To be completely sure everything is in order, consider having your will prepared by a trusts and estates attorney.

Having a will and probate are two entirely separate things. Yes, they both relate to events that happen after death. The difference is that a will allows the testator (the person writing the will) to record their wishes, whereas probate enables the personal representatives to action the testator's wishes.

2.7B. Living Wills

A living will or advanced directive is a legal instruction to refuse medical treatment if and when the time arrives. It spells out medical treatments you would and would not want to be used to keep you alive, as well as your preferences for other medical decisions, such as pain management or organ donation. In determining your wishes, think about your values.

You can write your will yourself, but you should get advice if your will is not straightforward. You need to get your will formally witnessed and signed to make it legally valid. If you want to update your will, you need to make an official alteration (called a 'codicil').

There are three main disadvantages to using a living will:

Living wills have a limited scope.

Living wills rely on a doctor's compliance.

Living wills are not always given to health care providers.

2.7C. Legacy Wills

Many charities in the UK offer a will writing service, in exchange for a small donation to their charity. It is an assumption when drafting the Will, a percentage of your estate will be donated to the said charity or an individual. These are commonly known as legacy wills. Many large national charities will have specialists in this market. Before entering into a legacy will for a specific charity, do some research and find out how much of your legacy will go to the charity, and how much will go in administration costs. The latter will sometimes make you want to rethink your potential donation.

2.7D. Probate

What is probate?

A much-used word in the legal system is 'Probate' but what exactly is probate.

Probate is the legal right to deal with someone's property, money and possessions (their 'estate') when they die.

You should not make any financial plans or put property on the market until you've got probate.

There are different probate rules in Scotland and Northern Ireland.

How to get probate

You need to apply to get probate. Before applying, you must check that it's needed and that you're eligible to apply. You also need to estimate and report the estate's value to find out if there's Inheritance Tax to pay. Probate can be applied for online and with relative ease. In some cases, it can take over 12 months to complete, and the fee is around £200.

A solicitor can be asked to act on your behalf, however this will be a lot more expensive, and you can expect to pay more than £2,000 or more, depending on how much work needs to be carried out.

Check if probate is needed.

Contact the financial organisations the person who died used (for example, their bank and mortgage company) to find out if you'll need probate to get access to their assets. Every organisation has its own rules.

You may not need probate if the person who died:

only had savings, at the time of writing this was set at a maximum of £50,000

owned shares or money with others - this automatically passes to the surviving owners unless they've agreed otherwise.

owned land or property as joint tenants with others - this automatically passes to the surviving owners.

Check if you can apply for probate.

Only certain people can apply for probate. Who can apply depends on whether or not there:

If there is a will, executors named in it can apply.

If there is not a will, then the closest living relative can apply.

2.7E. Cohabiting Couples

Unmarried and cohabiting partners have the legal right to claim against their partner's estate if they've been cohabiting for more than two years. However, they aren't automatically entitled to any of their partner's property, financial assets, or belongings unless they're jointly owned.

Cohabiting couples have no legal duty to support each other financially, either while you are living together or if you separate. Nor do you automatically share ownership of your possessions, savings, investments and so on. In general, ownership is unaffected by moving in together.

2.7F. Same Sex Couples

The Marriage (Same Sex Couples) Act of 2013 effectively puts same sex marriages on the same legal footing as those of heterosexual couples. The rights and obligations of a married same sex couple are exactly the same as those of a married opposite sex couple.

Pensions – when a same sex spouse dies, their partner is now entitled to a share of their pension that reflects the full number of years that the deceased paid into it. With a civil partnership the surviving spouse would only be entitled to a share of the pension based on contributions made since 2004 (for a private sector pension) or 1988 (for a public sector pension).

Recognition of their marital status in some foreign countries – increased countries are now accepting same sex marriages. Fewer countries recognise the legal status of a civil partnership.

Transgender issues – prior to the Same Sex Marriage Act of 2013, if a married heterosexual person underwent a sex change, their marriage would no longer be recognised after receiving their Gender Recognition Certificate. Therefore, people were sometimes being made to divorce and then enter into a civil partnership with their ex-spouse. The new law enables people in this situation to remain married and continue to have their marriage recognised.

The Married (Same Sex Couples) Act 2013 also enables civil partners to convert their partnership into a marriage if they wish.

2.7G. Civil Partnerships

In 2005 civil partnerships were introduced in the UK. Whilst sometimes referred to as 'gay marriage', this is not strictly accurate as there are legal differences between a civil partnership and a marriage.

The law describes a civil partnership as a legally registered relationship which offers same sex couples rights similar to those of married couples of the opposite sex. The legal rights relate to areas such as pensions, tax and the right to apply for parental responsibility for a partner's child.

When it comes to advising clients on civil partnerships there are a variety of legal services available, both before entering into a partnership and if a breakdown of the relationship occurs.

2.7H. Lasting Powers of Attorney (LPA)

A lasting power of attorney (LPA) is a legal document that lets you (the 'donor') appoint one or more people (known as 'attorneys') to help you make decisions or to make decisions on your behalf.

Overview

A lasting power of attorney (LPA) is a legal document that lets you (the 'donor') appoint one or more people (known as 'attorneys') to help you make decisions or to make decisions on your behalf. Due to the length of time it takes to set up LPA's, it is a wise move to create them earlier on in your retirement. They can then just be switched on figuratively speaking when they are needed.

This gives you more control over what happens to you if you have an accident or an illness and cannot make your own decisions (you 'lack mental capacity').

You must be 18 or over and have mental capacity (the ability to make your own decisions) when you make your LPA.

There are 2 types of LPA:

health and welfare

property and financial affairs

You can choose to make one type or both.

There's a different process in Scotland and Northern Ireland.

You do not need to live in the UK or be a British citizen.

How to make a lasting power of attorney

Choose your Attorney (you can have more than one) normally a family member.

Fill in the forms to appoint them as an attorney.

Register your LPA with the Office of the Public Guardian *(this can take up to 20 weeks).*

It currently costs £82 to register an LPA unless you get a reduction or exemption. The amount changes periodically

You can cancel your LPA if you no longer need it or want to make a new one.

Health and welfare lasting power of attorney

Use this LPA to give an attorney the power to make decisions about things like:

your daily routine, for example washing, dressing, eating.

medical care

moving into a care home

life-sustaining treatment

It can only be used when you're unable to make your own decisions.

Property and financial affairs lasting power of attorney

Use this LPA to give an attorney the power to make decisions about money and property for you, for example:

managing a bank or building society account

paying bills

collecting benefits or a pension

selling your home

It can be used as soon as it's registered, with your permission.

2.7J. Property Trusts

Inheritance Tax and settled property.

The act of putting an asset — such as money, land or buildings — into a trust is often known as 'making a settlement' or 'settling property'.

For Inheritance Tax purposes, each asset has its own separate identity. This means, for example, that one asset within a trust may be for the trustees to use at their discretion and therefore treated like a discretionary trust.

Another item within the same trust may be set aside for a disabled person and treated like a trust for a disabled person. In this case, there will be different Inheritance Tax rules for each asset.

Even though different assets may receive different tax treatment, it is always the total value of all the assets in a trust that is used to work out whether a trust exceeds the Inheritance Tax threshold and whether Inheritance Tax is due. There are different rules for distinct types of trust, and it is wise to seek expert guidance in such matters.

Inheritance Tax and excluded property.

Some assets are classed as excluded property and Inheritance Tax is not paid on them. However, the value of the assets may be brought in to calculate the rate of tax on certain exit charges and 10-year anniversary charges. Types of excluded property can include:

property situated outside the UK — that is owned by trustees and settled by someone who was permanently living outside the UK at the time of making the settlement.

government securities — known as FOTRA (free of tax to residents abroad)

The rules governing excluded property can be complicated.

Relevant property

Assets in a trust such as money, shares, houses or land are known as relevant property. Most property held in trusts counts as relevant property. Inheritance Tax may be due on the assets held within a trust when:

They are transferred out of a trust (exit charges)

A 10-year anniversary occurs.

The only exceptions to this rule are when the asset is:

In an interest in possession trust and it was put there before 22 March 2006

Subject to a 'transitional serial interest' made between 22 March 2006 and 5 October 2008

Put into an interest in possession trust by the terms of a will or the rules of intestacy.

Set aside for a disabled person.

Set aside for a bereaved minor.

Put into an age 18 to 25 trust.

Transfers into trust

A transfer of assets into a trust can include buildings, land or money and can be either of the following:

A gift made during a person's life.

A transfer or transaction that reduces the value of the settlor's estate (for example an asset is sold to trustees at less than its market value) — the loss to the person's estate is considered a gift or transfer.

Work out if Inheritance Tax is due.

For most types of trust Inheritance Tax is due when you make transfers that total more than the Inheritance Tax threshold of £325,000. You work this out by adding up the value of any transfers (based on the loss in value to the settlor's estate) and any chargeable gifts made in the previous 7 years by the settlor. Inheritance Tax is due on everything above the threshold.

If the trustees pay, the rate of tax is 20%. If the settlor pays the Inheritance Tax instead of the trustee, this means there will be an increased loss from the settlor's estate. The amount of tax due will therefore increase. These calculations are complex.

Death within 7 years of making a transfer.

If you die within 7 years of making a transfer into a trust your estate will have to pay Inheritance Tax at the full amount of 40%. This is instead of the reduced amount of 20% which is payable when the payment is made during your lifetime.

In this case your personal representative — who manages your estate when you die — will have to pay a further 20% out of your estate based on the value of the original transfer.

If no Inheritance Tax was due when you made the transfer, the value of the transfer is added to your estate when working out whether any Inheritance Tax is due.

If you make a gift into any type of trust but continue to benefit from the gift — for example, you give away your house but continue to live in it — you will pay 20% on the transfer and the gift will still count as part of your estate. These are known as gifts 'with reservation of benefit'.

This creates a situation where there are 2 possible Inheritance Tax charges if you die:

A charge when you transfer the gift into a trust.

a charge to your estate when you die — because the asset is still considered part of your estate.

To avoid double taxation, only the higher of these charges is applied — in other words you will never pay more than 40% Inheritance Tax.

Gifts into a trust for someone who is disabled.

You do not have to pay Inheritance Tax immediately if you make a gift to a trust for someone who is disabled but Inheritance Tax may still be due when you die.

The Inheritance Tax exit charge

Inheritance Tax is charged up to a maximum of 6% on assets — such as money, land or buildings — transferred out of a trust. This is known as an 'exit charge' and it's charged on all transfers of relevant property.

Transfers out of trust.

A transfer out of trust can occur when:

The trust comes to an end.

Some of the assets within the trust are distributed to beneficiaries.

A beneficiary becomes 'absolutely entitled' to enjoy an asset.

An asset becomes part of a 'special trust' (for example a charitable trust or trust for a disabled person) and it ceases to be 'relevant property'.

the trustees enter into a non-commercial transaction that reduces the value of the trust fund.

When there is no Inheritance Tax exit charge

There are some occasions when there's no Inheritance Tax exit charge — these apply even where the trust is a 'relevant property' trust. For instance, it is not charged:

on payments by trustees of costs or expenses incurred on assets held as relevant property

on some payments of capital to the beneficiary where Income Tax will be due

when the asset is transferred out of the trust within 3 months of setting up a trust, or within 3 months following a 10-year anniversary.

when assets are 'excluded property' — some foreign property is excluded property.

Calculating the Inheritance Tax exit charge

The calculations for the Inheritance Tax exit charge are complicated. You will need the following information before you can begin:

the value — before any Inheritance Tax Reliefs — of all the assets transferred into the trust in question, valued at the dates of transfer.

the value of all other transfers into other trusts made by the settlor on the same day as the trust in question was set up, valued at the date they were added.

the value of all transfers chargeable to Inheritance Tax that the settlor made in the 7 years before the trust in question was set up, valued at the date they were made.

Once you have this information there will be a different calculation depending on whether the:

transfer out of the trust occurs during the first 10 years of a trust's life.

transfer out occurs after the first 10 years.

trust is an 18 to 25 trust.

The 10-year anniversary charge

As a trustee, you will have to pay a charge on every 10-year anniversary of the date your trust was set up if your trust contains relevant property with a value above the Inheritance Tax threshold.

Work out the Inheritance Tax

Inheritance Tax is charged at each 10-year anniversary of the trust. It is charged on the net value of any relevant property in the trust on the day before that anniversary. Net value is the value after deducting any debts and reliefs such as Business or Agricultural Relief. There are different rules for trusts set up before 27th March 1974.

The calculation for the 10 yearly charge is complicated. Before you can begin, you'll need the following information:

the value of the relevant property in the trust on the day before the 10-year anniversary

the value — at the date it entered the trust — of any trust property that has not been relevant property at any time while in this trust.

the value of any property in any other trust (except wholly charitable trusts) that the settlor set up on the same date as this trust — use the value from the date it was set up

the value of any transfers subject to Inheritance Tax (whether into trusts or not) that the settlor made in the 7 years before this trust was set up — use the value at the date of transfer.

the value of any transfers — at the date they were transferred — of relevant property out of the trust within the last 10 years.

whether any of the relevant property was relevant property in the trust for less than the last 10 years

Dealing with a trust when someone dies

When someone dies, the job of managing their estate may involve dealing with trusts.

The person that has died may have wanted their assets put into trust when they die, or part of their estate may have already been held in trust.

The executor or administrator of the person's estate — known as the 'personal representative' — must find out the type of trust involved.

Inheritance Tax is due on everything above the Inheritance Tax threshold (£325,000 for the tax year 2021 to 2022). This can become more complicated when a trust is involved.

If a home is held in a trust or transferred to a trust when a person dies, the availability of the additional threshold will depend on the type of trust. This is because the type of trust will affect whether HM Revenue and Customs (HMRC) treat:

The home as part of a person's estate.

That person's direct descendants as inheriting the home.

When a home is held in a trust or transferred to a trust, you should discuss how the additional threshold applies with a solicitor or other professional adviser who knows about trust law.

There are 3 main ways that the deceased's personal representative may have to deal with a trust when working out whether Inheritance Tax is due.

When the deceased was the beneficiary of a trust

Some trusts are set up so that the beneficiary has ownership or a legal right to the income or assets in the trust. This will affect what is included in the estate of the beneficiary when they die.

A bare trust is one where the beneficiary is entitled to both the income and the assets in the trust. Therefore, when they die, both income and assets are considered part of their estate. The personal representative needs to work out whether there is any Inheritance Tax to pay and include the deceased's interest in the bare trust, on form IHT400 Inheritance Tax Account.

An interest in possession trust is one where the beneficiary is entitled to only the income from a trust. When they die, there are certain circumstances where the value of this 'interest in possession' is calculated as part of their estate. These include when the trust was set up:

before 22 March 2006

after 22 March 2006 and was either an 'immediate post death interest', a 'disabled person's interest' or a 'transitional serial interest' trust.

If you are the personal representative, you will need to work out the value of an 'interest in possession' and complete questions 45 and 75 on form IHT400. You'll need to liaise with the trustees to get this information. It is the trustees' duty to complete an IHT100 Inheritance Tax Account Form. This form must also be completed when an interest in possession trust comes to an end.

A home is included in a person's estate if it is either held in:

A bare trust

An interest in possession trust so that they had the right to use or occupy the property.

This can happen when a person is given a right to live in the family home following the death of their spouse. The home is held in trust for the lifetime of the beneficiary.

When the beneficiary dies, the estate will be eligible for the additional threshold if their direct descendants then inherit their home.

If the home is held in a discretionary trust, it would not normally be included in the beneficiary's estate. When the beneficiary dies, their estate will not be eligible for the additional threshold even if the home goes to the beneficiary's direct descendants.

When the deceased transferred assets into a trust before they died

There may have been an Inheritance Tax charge of 20% when assets were transferred into a discretionary trust. If you are the personal representative, you must find out whether the deceased made any transfers into a trust in the 7 years before they died. If they did, and they paid Inheritance Tax at that time, the tax will be recalculated at 40% and a credit allowed for the tax paid when the trust was set up. The trustees will be liable to pay the extra tax. You must show this on form IHT400 at question 28.

Even if no Inheritance Tax is due on the transfer you may need to add its value to the deceased's estate when you are working out the value for Inheritance Tax purposes.

The additional threshold will not apply to transfers of a home or any other assets to a discretionary trust before a person died. This applies even if the beneficiary is a direct descendant or if they are entitled to the assets in the trust.

When a trust is set up by a will

Someone might ask in their will that some or all of their assets are placed in a trust. A trust set up under these circumstances is known as a 'will trust'. The personal representative must then make sure that the trust is set up properly and all taxes are paid on assets going into it.

If a home is put into an interest in possession trust at the time someone dies, the added threshold will be available for their estate if the person who receives help from the trust is their direct descendant.

If the beneficiary is not a direct descendant, the estate will not qualify for the added threshold. In that case the unused added threshold would be available to o transfer to a surviving spouse or civil partners estate.

A great way (and on many occasions neglected) to keep everything together is 'The Black Box' system. Whilst researching this publication we found that many do not everything that they should about what will happen after loved ones pass away. Stories have been heard of people who have no will, a will that has not been signed or witnessed, secret bank accounts, properties that partners are unaware of, the list goes on.

A great way of keeping everything in one place is a simple metal filing box 'The Black Box'. In this box every relevant document can be stored that needs to be actioned after your death. Although not endless, here are a few suggestions of what should be in the box:

Wills and Trust Documents.

Your funeral arrangements.

Details of Insurances and Bonds

Property Deeds.

Details of Bank Accounts, Savings and Investments.

Details of Pensions the need transferring.

Direct Debits from Banks.

Utility provider.

Online passwords and account numbers.

Mobile phone and laptop passwords.

Keys to safety deposit boxes.

Details of family heirlooms that may be in safe storage.

But above all tell your partner and loved ones where to find this information. They will be grieving after your demise and if you can reduce the heartache in some small way, it has got to be of benefit to all concerned.

2.8A. Care Homes

2.8B. Care at Home or Carer Support

2.8C. Hospices

2.8 Care and Carers

Health care is described as various levels of care: primary, secondary, tertiary, and quaternary.

In medicine, levels of care refer to the complexity of the medical cases doctors treat and the skills and specialties of the providers. Levels are divided into four categories.

Primary care is when you consult with your primary care provider. *Secondary care* is when you see a specialist such as an oncologist or endocrinologist. *Tertiary care* refers to specialized care in a hospital setting such as dialysis or heart surgery. *Quaternary care* is an advanced level of specialized care, for example cancer care.

As a patient, you might sometimes hear these terms. So, knowing their definitions can help you better understand what your doctor is talking about and help you recognize the level of care you're receiving or going to need.

2.8A. Care Homes

Care homes supply accommodation and personal care for people who need extra support in their daily lives. Personal care might include help with eating, washing, dressing, going to the toilet or taking medication. Some care homes also offer social activities such as day trips or outings.

There are two main types of care homes:

Residential Care - Care homes without nursing care. If the person has any nursing needs, help may be provided by the District Nursing Service visiting whenever they are needed.

Nursing Care - Care homes with nursing care. Qualified nursing staff are on duty 24 hours per day.

2.8B. Care at Home or Carer Support

Having a paid carer to come and visit you in your own home can make an enormous difference to the way you live your life. More so if you have mobility issues, or difficulty getting around. A home carer can help to you to remain at home and live independently. This type of care is known as homecare or domiciliary care, occasionally people refer to it as a home help.

A home help from a paid carer can cost around £20 per hour at the time of drafting this book, but it varies to where you live in the country. On some occasions your local council will aid you with or contribute towards to cost.

This is heavily dependent on you own personal financial circumstances. Homecare can be very flexible and is tailored to your own personal needs. You may need a paid carer for only an hour a week, or sometimes several hours a day. Live in carers are also available, again dependent on your own personal needs. Homecare can also be on a temporary basis to help you after an illness or can be long term due to a disability. Home adaptations or household gadgets may also be a consideration to make your life easier.

When should I consider assistance from a paid carer?

You may wish to consider care in the home if:

You are finding it difficult to cope with daily routines, such as washing, dressing and getting out and about.

You do not want to move into a care home and continue to live independently.

You can still get about your home, and it is safe for you to live in, or can be adapted to make it safe.

A paid carer can visit you in your home and aid you with many things, some examples are:

Getting out of bed in the morning.

Washing and dressing.

Showering, washing and brushing your hair.

Using the toilet.

Preparing meals and drinks.

Helping with medications.

Fetching prescriptions and shopping.

Getting you out to social events.

Preparing you for bed.

How can a Home Help assist me?

A home help is slightly different to homecare, and generally means day to day domestic tasks that you may need help with, for example:

Cleaning and bed making

Washing crockery etc.

Doing the laundry

Gardening

Shopping

Some councils may offer this, but most do not offer a home help service due to financial constraints. Contact local and national charities such as The Royal Voluntary Service, The British Red Cross, or your local branch of Age UK to see if they can help. They may require a financial contribution and are not always free.

How can I get help from a paid carer?

Your local council can arrange homecare for you if you are eligible for it. They normally carry out a survey and a means test first.

If you want the council to help you with homecare, start by asking them to carry out a needs assessment, this will help them to decide whether you are eligible.

You can arrange your own homecare from a private company. Local authorities will have a register of those in your area. Be cautious of those who approach you directly.

Paying for Homecare

Depending on your own personal circumstances, your local council may contribute to the cost of your homecare, alternatively you will have to pay for it yourself.

If your needs assessment recommends homecare, you may be able to get some aid from the local council to help with the cost.

When a council is paying all or some of the cost of your homecare, they must give you a care and support plan. A sort of contract of what you should receive.

You may decide to opt for a personal budget as a direct payment each month. This choice gives you the control to employ someone you know to care for you at home rather than using a homecare agency. Opting for this may make you an employer of your carer with other responsibilities that you do not want.

If you do not qualify for any council contribution towards homecare costs, then you will have to pay the full cost yourself.

Government Benefits that can help with your homecare.

Firstly, check if you are eligible for any benefits, such as attendance allowance, or PIP personal independence payments, these are not means tested and can help towards the costs of homecare. It is wise to keep up to date with the benefits available as they do change from time to time.

2.8C. Hospices

A Hospice is provided for a person with a terminal illness whose doctor believes he or she has six months or less to live if the illness runs its natural course.

Most Hospices in the UK are run as independent charities, but still work closely with local medical authorities.

2.9A. Deciding Your Final Moment

It has been said that many people know when they are going to die, with every emotion going on within a family group it is rarely talked about. A time comes in life when the body starts to fail followed by the mind, then the stages of death are remarkably close.

Choosing the moment to die. Thinking about the last hours and moments of life is hard but knowing what to expect may ease some of the worries you may be having. Everyone's experiences are different but there are changes that often happen near to someone's death that may be signs the person is dying.

It may be reassuring to know that for many people with a terminal illness, their needs are met in the last couple of days and the ultimate moments are peaceful.

Here are some changes that sometimes happen shortly before a person dies:

Loss of consciousness - Many people lose consciousness near the end of life. But they may still have some awareness of other people in the room. They may be able to hear what's being said or feel someone holding their hand.

Changes to skin - Limbs, hands and feet may feel colder. This is because the blood circulation is slowing down.

People with lighter skin tones may look slightly blue or their skin can become mottled (have different coloured blotches or patches).

On people with darker skin tones, blue can be hard to see. It may be easier to see on their lips, nose, cheeks, ears, tongue, or the inside of their mouth. Mottling is also harder to see on darker skin tones – it might look darker than normal, purple or brownish in colour.

Noisy breathing - Breathing may become loud and noisy if mucous has built up in the airways. This is because the person isn't coughing or clearing their airways. Some people call this type of breathing the death rattle because it can happen in the last days or hours of life.

It can be upsetting or worrying for those around the person to hear their noisy breathing. But it's unlikely to be painful or distressing for the person who's dying. Often, they will be unconscious or won't be aware of it.

Shallow or irregular breathing - As the moment of death comes nearer, breathing usually slows down and becomes irregular. It might stop and then start again or there might be long pauses or stops between breaths. This is known as Cheyne-Stokes breathing. This can last for a brief time or long time before breathing finally stops.

In recent years some countries have allowed the act of euthanasia to take place under medical supervision. This is normally for people who have a lifelong debilitating illness or physical handicap. Euthanasia, also called mercy killing, act or practice of painlessly putting to death persons suffering from painful and incurable disease or incapacitating physical disorder or allowing them to die by withholding treatment or withdrawing artificial life-support measures. There are 4 main types of euthanasia, i.e., active, passive, indirect, and physician-assisted suicide. Typically, a peaceful death takes 30 seconds from intravenous euthanasia solution administration.

Euthanasia is illegal and could be prosecuted as murder or manslaughter. 'Assisting or encouraging' another person's suicide is prohibited by s. 2 of the Suicide Act 1961, as amended by the Coroners and Justice Act 2009. The Director of Public Prosecutions (DPP) examines individual cases to decide whether to prosecute.

Assisted suicide is the act of deliberately aiding another person to kill themselves. If a relative of a person with a terminal illness obtained strong sedatives, knowing the person intended to use them to kill themselves, the relative may be considered to be aiding suicide.

The Law in Great Britain in Relation to Euthanasia

Both euthanasia and assisted suicide are illegal under English law. In recent years, much lobbying has been carried out to change the law in relation to euthanasia. However, at the time of drafting this book, the current law states that:

Assisted suicide is illegal under the terms of the Suicide Act (1961) and is punishable by up to 14 years' imprisonment. Trying to kill yourself is not a criminal act.

Depending on the circumstances, euthanasia is regarded as either manslaughter or murder. The maximum penalty is life imprisonment.

2.9C. Palliative Care

Palliative care is about improving the quality of life of anyone facing a life-threatening condition. It includes physical, emotional and spiritual care.

End of life care is support for people in the last weeks, months or even years of their life. It should help you to live as well as possible until the time comes to die, and you should be able to die with dignity.

The people providing your care should ask you about your preferences and wishes, these are then taken into account and help to work out your care plan. The care plan should also support your family, and others important to you.

You have a legal right to express your wishes about where you would like to receive your care and also where you want to die. Practicalities relating to your own personal circumstances sometime can dictate this decision. You can receive end of life care at home, in a care home, hospice or in a hospital, this is much dependent on your needs as well as your personal preference.

Everyone who is approaching the end of their life are entitled to high quality care, irrespective of where they are being cared for.

2.9D. The Funeral Director, Burials and Cremations

In the UK, the Funeral Director often referred to as an Undertaker, will normally arrange everything that you need for your Funeral. Whether or not it is a burial or a cremation, their job is to carry out the wishes of the deceased. Funerals can either be paid for in advance with a pre-paid funeral bond or in arrears by the family. In some cases, the state may pay for a funeral, but only if no assets are left by the deceased, this is sometimes referred to as a pauper's funeral.

How does a burial work?

Burial, also known as interment or inhumation, is a method of final disposition whereby a dead body is placed into the ground, sometimes with objects. This is usually carried out by excavating a pit or trench, placing the deceased and objects in it, and covering it over. The graveyard that the burial takes place in is usually owned by a district council or by a church.

What happens during a cremation?

A human Cremation is a process that uses intense heat to turn the remains of a deceased person into ashes. The cremation process takes place in a specially designed cremation chamber which holds one deceased person and exposes them to intense heat for a period of around two hours. At a later date after the cremation has taken place the ashes of the deceased are normally offered to a family relative.

In recent years the offer of Direct Funerals has become more common. This is where the deceased in taken for cremation without any formal service and normally with no relatives present.

2.9E. Direct Funerals

A fast-growing alternative to traditional funerals in the UK are Direct Funerals. A direct burial or cremation will take place without a ceremony or service beforehand, and usually without any mourners present. Direct funerals include only the essential elements of a cremation or burial enabling the funeral provider to keep costs to a minimum. A few companies in the UK specialise in this market, Companies such as Simplicity Cremations https://www.simplicity.co.uk/

and Pure Cremations https://www.purecremation.co.uk/ many other companies offer a similar service.

Types of religious are generally dictated by your cultural beliefs and religion, and the religious ceremony will follow guidelines dictated by each faith. But like everything in life, even in death you have a choice. It is for that very reason that you inform your relatives of your choice before you die. After you have passed on it is too late to assume the family knew of your wishes and got it right.

Death by Suspicious or Unusual Circumstances

On occasions a person may die for no apparent reason and the body may then be referred to a coroner's office to establish the cause of death. When this occurs, the family will not be able to carry out a funeral until the body of the deceased is released. After an autopsy has been carried out the body is normally released.

What is an autopsy?

A post-mortem examination, also known as an autopsy, is the examination of a body after death. The aim of a post-mortem is to determine the cause of death. Post-mortems are carried out by pathologists (doctors who specialise in understanding the nature and causes of disease).

It is an indictable offence at common law to prevent the lawful and decent burial of a dead body and it is also an offence at common law to obstruct a coroner by disposing of a dead body in order to prevent an inquest being held upon it. Both of these offences are punishable by fine and imprisonment at the discretion of the court.

2.9G. Bereavement & Counselling

After losing a close relative or partner is most important to go through bereavement and get some counselling to help you with the grieving process. It may sound very clinical but dealing with grief will always be very traumatic and many people and experts are there to help.

What is bereavement?

Bereavement is the experience of losing someone important to us. It is characterised by grief, which is the process and the range of emotions we go through as we gradually adjust to the loss. Losing someone important to us can be emotionally devastating - whether that be a partner, family member, friend or pet.

What is counselling?

Counselling is a collaborative effort between the counsellor and client. Professional counsellors help clients find goals and potential solutions to problems which cause emotional turmoil; look to improve communication and coping skills; strengthen self-esteem; and promote behaviour change and best mental health. Counselling is a process of talking about and working through your personal problems with a counsellor. The counsellor helps you to address your problems in a positive way by helping you to clarify the issues, explore options, develop strategies, and increase self-awareness.

2.9H. After You Partner Has Gone

It is an inevitable fact of life that eventually your long-term partner will pass away. Some couple even joke about who will go first. As much as we prepare ourselves for this day, it will still come as a shock.

What You May Feel

The event might be expected after a long-term illness, it might just happen without warning, whichever way it occurs will create a large amount of different emotions. Some obvious and others that will be difficult to comprehend. The death of a spouse or long-term partner will often be a confusing experience, you may be shocked, confused, sad, relieved or maybe feel nothing at all. After a long illness relief is often an expected reaction to someone close passing away.

In the event that you have had a difficult relationship with your former partner, you may feel a longing or regret that you had not done things differently. When someone dies, support is often focused on the offspring of the person and not directly at the surviving partner, who possibly has been the head of the family, and people expect them to be able to deal with the problem. This invariably is never the case.

Your Health

It may sound easy to say but it is important to look after yourself whilst you are grieving. You own health and wellbeing are still of great importance.

Memorials

Your relationship with the deceased carries on after a partner dies. The memory of them carries on and does not die. It can help you through the grieving process if you continue your routines as if they were still alive. Organising a permanent memorial to them in your home may be a way of helping you to deal with the loss. Or a special event for everyone that knew your partner to honour their life.

Reminders

Anniversaries, holidays, birthday, and special days will be difficult times for you think ahead as to how you are going to deal with these days and talk about them in advance with families and friends.

Moving On and New Relationships

A difficult subject straight after having lost a loved one that you may have spent a large amount of your life with. You may feel pressured by friends and family to find someone new. Alternatively, family may well be opposed to the very idea of it. The decision should be yours and yours alone, but only if you feel it is right for you. Some people do this quickly, others take their time, and many never entertain the idea, and accept a life of solitude.

You may be guided by your family to relocate to somewhere in close proximity to them. Again, it should be your decision, and yours alone. Weigh up all of the pros and cons of such a move, and what it will mean for your circle of friends, who may be your support group.

Above all there will always be help out there and ask for help when you need it. The worst-case scenario is becoming a recluse and dying of loneliness because you were too proud to ask.

3.1 Top Tips for Retirement

3.2 References, Future Reading and Links

3.1 Top Tips for Retirement

We have drawn up a list of Top Tips for your retirement, they are not rated in any particular order, and we think they are all of equal importance.

Set up your pension at the earliest opportunity.

Understand what your pension will deliver.

Buy a funeral bond when you can afford it.

Plan to enter retirement debt free.

If possible, keep a rainy-day savings fund.

Live within your financial means, and budget accordingly.

Only use credit if it can be paid off monthly.

Create a Black Box. See section 2.7K

If you own property, consider a family trust.

Remember you need to apply for state pension, it is not automatically granted.

Ensure you claim all benefits that you are entitled to.

Keep fit and try to keep you BMI below 25.

Eat a healthy diet.

Keep your alcohol intake low and within medical guidelines.

Keep communication fluid with relatives.

If you are lonely – ask for help and join a local group.

Get a hobby or pastime.

Accept your limitations.

Be aware of age-related illnesses and get help when needed.

Make sure you have a will and tell people where it is kept.

If you are unwell, seek medical attention.

3.2 References, Future Reading and Links

Pension Planning

https://nationalpensionadvisors.co.uk/

https://www.moneyhelper.org.uk/

https://www.gov.uk/state-pension

https://www.gov.uk/government/publications/state-pension-age-timetable/state-pension-age-timetable

Retirement Planning

https://www.unbiased.co.uk/

https://www.fisherinvestments.com/

Estate Planning

https://www.ageuk.org.uk/

Funeral Planning

https://www.dignityfunerals.co.uk/

Money Matters, Insurances and Investment Scams

https://www.moneyhelper.org.uk/

Benefits and Government Assistance

https://www.ageuk.org.uk/information-advice/money-legal/benefits-entitlements/

Part Time Work

https://restless.co.uk/

First Aid and Preventing Accidents

https://www.rospa.com/

Blood Donation and Organ Donations

https://www.blood.co.uk/

Age Related Medical Conditions

https://www.ageuk.org.uk/

Dementia & Parkinson's Disease

https://www.dementiauk.org/

https://www.parkinsons.org.uk/

Loneliness & Depression

https://www.relate.org.uk/

Personal Mobility

https://www.motability.co.uk/how-it- works/allowances/pip/

Government Assistance

https://www.gov.uk/benefits-calculators

Aids to Living Safely at Home

https://www.nhs.uk/conditions/social-care-and-support-guide/

Wills

https://www.gov.uk/make-will

Probate

https://www.gov.uk/applying-for-probate

Lasting Powers of Attorney

https://www.gov.uk/power-of-attorney

Property Trusts

https://www.gov.uk/guidance/trusts-and-inheritance-tax

Care and Carers

https://www.carersuk.org/

Care Homes

https://www.carehome.co.uk/

Direct Funerals

https://directfuneral.co.uk/

https://www.dignityfunerals.co.uk/

Bereavement & Counselling

https://www.relate.org.uk/

After Your Partner Has Gone

https://www.cruse.org.uk/

You may be interested in other books by the same Other Books by the same Author -

ISBN 978-1-5272-4308-8 A Military Chefs Journey

ISBN 978-1-5272-4696-6 Cooking Made Simple

ISBN 979-8-6416-2683-3 A Survival Guide to Home Cooking

ISBN 979-8-6447-8635-0 A Survival Guide to British Catchphrases

All are available on Amazon.